D1063910

Legendary Rock Band

Other Titles in

REBELS OF ROCK

Library Ed.
ISBN-13: 978-0-7660-3031-2
Paperback
ISBN-13: 978-0-7660-3623-9

Library Ed.
ISBN-13: 978-0-7660-3028-2
Paperback
ISBN-13: 978-0-7660-3620-8

Library Ed.
ISBN-13: 978-0-7660-3029-9
Paperback
ISBN-13: 978-0-7660-3621-5

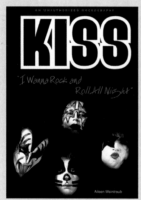

Library Ed.
ISBN-13: 978-0-7660-3027-5
Paperback
ISBN-13: 978-0-7660-3619-2

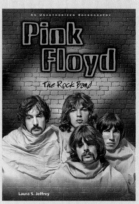

Library Ed.
ISBN-13: 978-0-7660-3030-5
Paperback
ISBN-13: 978-0-7660-3622-2

LED ZEPPELIN

Legendary Rock Band

Michael A. Schuman

REBELS OF **ROCK**

Enslow Publishers, Inc.
40 Industrial Road
Box 398
Berkeley Heights, NJ 07922
USA

http://www.enslow.com

TO PATTI, WITH "ALL OF MY LOVE"

Library of Congress Cataloging-in-Publication Data

Schuman, Michael.
    Led Zeppelin : legendary rock band / Michael A. Schuman.
        p. cm. — (Rebels of rock)
    Includes bibliographical references, discography, and index.
    ISBN-13: 978-0-7660-3026-8 (library ed.)
    ISBN-10: 0-7660-3026-1 (library ed.)
    1. Led Zeppelin (Musical group)—Juvenile literature. 2. Rock musicians—England—Biography—Juvenile literature. I. Title.
    ML3930.L32S38 2010
    782.42166092'2—dc22
                                                     2008017433

ISBN-13: 978-0-7660-3618-5 (paperback ed.)
ISBN-10: 0-7660-3618-9 (paperback ed.)

Printed in the United States of America

10 9 8 7 6 5 4 3 2 1

To Our Readers: This book has not been authorized by Led Zeppelin or its successors.

We have done our best to make sure all Internet Addresses in this book were active and appropriate when we went to press. However, the author and the publisher have no control over and assume no liability for the material available on those Internet sites or on other Web sites they may link to. Any comments or suggestions can be sent by e-mail to comments@enslow.com or to the address on the back cover.

Every effort has been made to locate all copyright holders of material used in this book. If any errors or omissions have occurred, corrections will be made in future editions of this book.

♻ Enslow Publishers, Inc., is committed to printing our books on recycled paper. The paper in every book contains 10% to 30% post-consumer waste (PCW). The cover board on the outside of each book contains 100% PCW. Our goal is to do our part to help young people and the environment too!

Photo Credits: Jorgen Angel/Redferns, p. 35; Associated Press, pp. 58, 89 (top and bottom); Ian Dickson/Redferns, p. 32; Ian Dickson/Rex Features/Courtesy Everett Collection, p. 55; Everett Collection, p. 69; GAB Archives/Redferns, pp. 19, 74; Exclusive by Getty Images, pp. 9, 87; Frank Griffin/LFI, p. 63; ILPO MUSTO/Rex Features/Courtesy Everett Collection, p. 14; John S. Mason, p. 46; Michael Ochs Archives/Getty Images, p. 38; Ed Robinson/Redferns, p. 6; Peter Still/Redferns, p. 27; Time & Life Pictures/Getty Images, p. 43; WireImage/Getty Images, pp. 21, 81.

Cover Photo: Everett Collection. Led Zeppelin in 1973.

CONTENTS

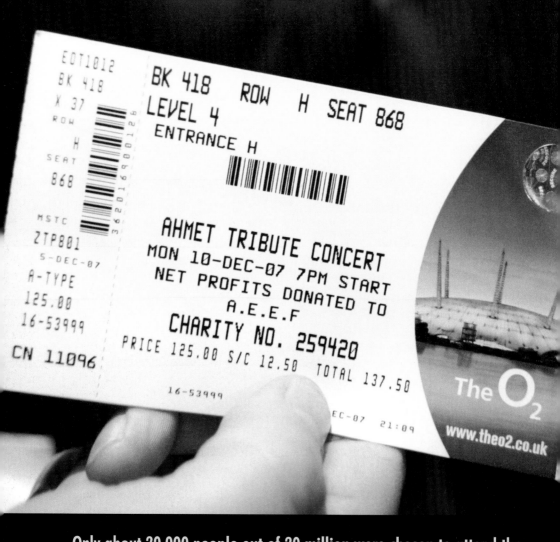

Only about 20,000 people out of 20 million were chosen to attend the Ahmet Tribute Concert in which Led Zeppelin was performing.

1

"THE GREATEST MOMENT OF MY LIFE"

No one knew what to expect from Led Zeppelin's first full concert in what seemed an eternity. They had formed in 1968 and dominated the music scene in the 1970s. The band had last performed together publicly in a brief and poorly reviewed set in 1987.

But now it was 2007. The three original band members were nearing or over sixty years old. Could they still play rock and roll? Could they still command the stage?

In their prime, their shows had been spectacular. The quartet was once the face of rock music. Some said they were the world's first heavy metal band. In their heyday they had wild manes of hair down to their shoulders or longer. Dozens of their songs are rock classics, including "Stairway to Heaven," "Whole Lotta Love," and "Misty Mountain Hop."

There was a lot of pressure in the weeks prior to the 2007 concert. Expectations were high. One critic wrote, "For sure, it's THE music event of the year, of the decade even. Let's hope Led Zeppelin are still climbing that Stairway to Heaven."[1]

Another reporter wrote three days before the big event: "They have all the ingredients to make a great performance and they have a dedicated fan-base, but with this much of a break and with so much to live up to, can they really fulfill the expectations?"[2]

It was estimated that about twenty million people entered a lottery for the roughly twenty thousand available seats.[3] These included fans who grew up with Zeppelin as well as those who were not even born when the group split up. It also included people from across the world.

A fifteen-year-old boy from Tucson, Arizona, named Zack Briefer was one of the few who won a pair of tickets through the lottery. Zack's father, Andy, said he saw Zack crying on his bedroom floor the morning Zack found out he won the tickets. Andy said, "I ran into his room and said 'What's wrong?' He [Zack] said, 'This is the greatest moment of my life.'"[4]

Led Zeppelin decided to do this concert for a special reason. It was a charity performance dedicated to the founder of

Atlantic Records, Ahmet Ertegun. Ertegun had died the previous year, and Led Zeppelin owed their career to his record company. Zeppelin was first signed by Atlantic Records. Money earned from this concert would go to the Ahmet Ertegun Education Fund. The charity provides scholarships to needy students in the United States, Great Britain, and Ertegun's home country, Turkey.

At the first rehearsals, singer Robert Plant said he was

ON DECEMBER 10, 2007, LED ZEPPELIN PERFORMED IN LONDON, ENGLAND.

worried whether his fifty-nine-year-old voice could still belt out songs. Lead guitarist Jimmy Page confessed about the first rehearsal, "It was a bit nervy. I really wanted it to work. I didn't want to be the one who couldn't do it."[5]

As they took the stage on the O_2 Arena outside London on December 10, 2007, the rock and roll rabble-rousers hardly looked like they did in their prime. Jimmy Page had turned completely gray. Bass player John Paul Jones had cropped his hair to the point that he could pass for a British businessman. Robert Plant's blond hair was still shoulder length, but his face was lined with the wrinkles of middle age. Even the drummer, Jason Bonham, was in his forties. Bonham was the son of Zeppelin's original drummer, John Bonham, who died in 1980. It was John Bonham's death that caused the band to break up.

Zeppelin opened with the song "Good Times Bad Times," the same song they opened with during concerts decades ago. The fact that they did not look the same or move as fast did not bother the full house. Music critic Ben Ratliff wrote, "As for Mr. Page, his guitar solos weren't as frenetic and articulated as they used to be, but that only drove home the point that they were always secondary to the riffs, which on Monday were enormous, nasty, glorious."[6]

The concert lasted about two hours, and Zeppelin performed sixteen of their best-known numbers.

The verdict from fans and critics alike was the same:

so many years had passed but Led Zeppelin could still rock. One reporter wrote, "You might think it couldn't possibly live up to expectations, but, it transpires, the opposite is in fact true of Led Zeppelin's first public appearance in [twenty] years."[7]

Another reporter wrote that Zeppelin's singer had nothing to worry about concerning his aging voice. The review said, "Plant sounds fantastic, and retains an utterly magnetic and startlingly lithe presence on stage . . ."[8]

A thirty-nine-year-old British fan named Mary Wallace said, "Jimmy Page was incredible tonight. If anything, I think his guitar playing has got better over the years."[9]

Perhaps the feeling of most fans was best summed up by a fan named Andreas from Norway. Andreas posted on a BBC (British Broadcasting Company) Web site, "There is only one thing I can really say about the concert. I can die happily now."[10]

IN THE BAND

The members of Led Zeppelin were all products of England, and they had one thing in common: a love of music. In their early years, that specifically meant American blues and rock and roll.

Jimmy Page

Jimmy Page was born on January 9, 1944, in the town of Heston not far from England's capital, London. His full name is James Patrick Page. When he was a boy, his parents moved to a town called Feltham. Feltham is so close to Heathrow Airport outside London that it seemed to him at times that the noisy airplanes were landing inside his house.

As a boy Jimmy liked fishing and collecting stamps. He was also a pretty good hurdler and starred in school track meets. In school, his favorite subject was art. But Jimmy's parents thought there was no way anyone could make a living as an artist. According to Page, "they thought [art] was a loser's game."[1]

Despite his parents' objections, he was not ready to give up on art. Then in 1956, when Jimmy was twelve, he found another passion.

Rock and roll music was brand-new. It appealed to young people, and was taking over the music scene like a rocket. There were several stars, but the biggest of all was Elvis Presley. Elvis played guitar and sang with either a two- or three-piece band behind him.

Presley was a rebel, and that attracted 1950s teenagers. However, his acts of rebellion were very mild by today's standards. Presley was a white man, but became famous for recording songs such as "Hound Dog," originally written for an African-American singer named Willie Mae "Big Mama" Thornton. Around that time he had hit records with other songs arranged in the same style, including "Heartbreak Hotel" and "Blue Suede Shoes." This was a time of legal segregation, or separation of the races, and the idea of white teenagers listening to music with black roots was scary to many white adults.

Presley swiveled his hips while playing his guitar and

Jimmy Page playing guitar with a violin bow

singing. That action seemed suggestive to adults. Presley wore his hair in a ducktail, a style in which the hair is combed back at the sides to meet at one point in the back. A teenage boy in Michigan was expelled from high school in 1956 for wearing an Elvis-style haircut.[2]

On the other hand, Presley did not spit in the face of authority. He referred to elders as "Sir" and "Ma'am" and rarely if ever swore. When some television hosts asked Presley to tone down his hip movements on their programs, he willingly did so.

None of that stopped teenagers from admiring him. Girls wished they could date him. Boys wanted to be like him.

Jimmy Page got caught up in the Elvis frenzy. One Elvis record he especially liked was titled *Baby, Let's Play House*. Page was impressed by Presley's rich voice, but even more interested in the guitar work. Presley played lead, and Scotty Moore and James Burton played rhythm guitar and stand-up bass. Jimmy played that record over and over until he nearly wore it out. Page said, "I just sort of heard two guitars and bass and thought, 'Yeah, I want to be part of this.' There was so much energy and vitality coming out of it."[3]

Like many boys then, Page bought a guitar so he could try to be the next Elvis. He also bought a self-help guitar instruction book titled *Play in a Day*. Unlike other boys who wanted to play like Elvis but were not talented, Jimmy was skilled with the guitar.

Aside from teaching himself guitar, Page continued to spend much of his spare time dabbling in art. After graduating from public school, he was torn between pursuing music or art as a career. He jammed and formed pickup groups with friends and other musicians he met. While playing in a local dance hall called the Marquee, Jimmy was spotted by a singer named Neil Christian. Neil was the lead singer in a band called Neil Christian and the Crusaders. Neil was impressed by Jimmy's guitar-playing ability and asked him to join the Crusaders to play at gigs, or appearances, in different parts of England.

Neil was a courteous young man, and asked Jimmy's parents if they would allow their son to tour with his band. If it meant that Jimmy would give up art, Jimmy's father was okay with it. The Crusaders kept a hectic schedule. They would play a gig, then travel in a van to a different town for another one. The van had seen better days and would often break down on the road. The constant travel and long hours took a toll on Page.

He said, "I remember one night walking outside a gig, and the next point waking up and I was laying on the floor in some sort of dressing room. I just collapsed and couldn't keep going, and it was just fatigue and exhaustion. . . . I was getting ill, and I really thought 'I just can't carry on.'"[4]

Page decided to take a break from traveling with the Crusaders and enroll in art school. That was fine for Page,

since the Crusaders never grew into a big-time band. Page spent his time in and out of school painting and drawing. But no matter how much he tried he could not stay away from his guitar. He hung around London music clubs such as the Marquee and another called Crawdaddy. He would jam, or play unrehearsed music, with any musicians who were around. If he was not jamming Elvis songs, he was doing so to tunes by American rock guitarist Gene Vincent or African-American rock and roll pioneers Chuck Berry and Bo Diddley.

In time he was hired as a session musician. Session musicians play instruments in the background for more famous musicians. They rarely tour and do almost all their work in recording studios. Because they play in the background they are usually unknown to most music buyers.

Page finally gave up art and became a full-time session musician. For about six years he played background for a variety of performers. Not surprisingly, he played behind hot rock bands the Rolling Stones and the Kinks. However, he also played behind performers one would never have expected him to team up with. These included Petula Clark and Burt Bacharach. That would be similar today to Billie Joe Armstrong of Green Day playing backup for Celine Dion or Clay Aiken.

The fact that Jimmy could not read music was a problem at first. He said that when he first saw sheet music it looked like crows on telephone wires. In fact, he was a bit self-conscious

as he sometimes made mistakes trying to follow the printed music. Gradually, he taught himself to read music and became known as a superb studio musician.

After so many years Page became tired of playing background for others. He was not allowed to improvise, or to add even a bit of his own style. Out of frustration, Jimmy began looking for other outlets for his talent. In 1965, he released a single record, or "45," titled "She Just Satisfies." Before the days of compact discs, music companies released small two-sided records that contained only one song on each side. These were known as singles. Because they moved at forty-five revolutions per minute, they were also known as 45s. Each had an "A" side and a "B" side. The song on the "A" side was the one meant for radio stations to play.

"She Just Satisfies" was released as the "A" side of Page's single. Unfortunately, it sold very few copies.

Around that time Page was given an opportunity to work as a record producer. It was a new adventure and led to a major contact. While in the recording studio he met another guitarist, Eric Clapton.

Clapton was the lead guitarist of the Yardbirds, a blues-rock band. In 1965, Clapton quit the Yardbirds and suggested that Page fill his position. Because he had had health problems traveling with Neil Christian and the Crusaders, Jimmy was hesitant to play with a band that would have to tour. So the Yardbirds hired a different lead guitarist, Jeff Beck.

In June 1966, Page was given another chance to join the Yardbirds, but as a bass guitarist. By now the Yardbirds had had several hit singles in Great Britain and the United States. Page took the chance and joined the band. When rhythm guitarist Chris Dreja switched to bass, Page was free to play the lead guitar he loved. He and Beck shared lead guitar roles.

JIMMY PAGE WAS ASKED TO JOIN THE YARDBIRDS (FROM LEFT TO RIGHT: CHRIS DREJA, JIMMY PAGE, JIM MCCARTY, KEITH RELF, AND JEFF BECK).

The trouble was that the Yardbirds were starting to fall apart as a group. Some members were abusing alcohol and other drugs. As a result, their performances were suffering. It seemed as if Page was the only band member concerned about the quality of the Yardbirds' work.[5] The Yardbirds officially split up in 1968.

Despite the problems, Page enjoyed his two-year stint with the Yardbirds. He said, "Any musician would have jumped at the chance to play in that band."[6]

Robert Plant

Singer Robert Anthony Plant is over four years younger than Jimmy Page. He was born August 20, 1948, and grew up in Kidderminster, a suburb of Birmingham in central England. His father, Robert, Sr., made a comfortable living as a civil engineer. He wanted his son to go into a career more respectable than music. Robert Jr. was a good student who loved to read. However, music was his passion.

He could also play the role of a class clown. Once, when Robert was in grade school, he hid a pair or tennis shoes inside the school piano. The teacher found it impossible to play the instrument. When it was discovered that Robert was behind the prank, he was expelled from music class. That hurt, since it was Robert's favorite class.

Like Jimmy Page, Robert idolized Elvis Presley. He would stand in front of a mirror in his home trying his hardest to

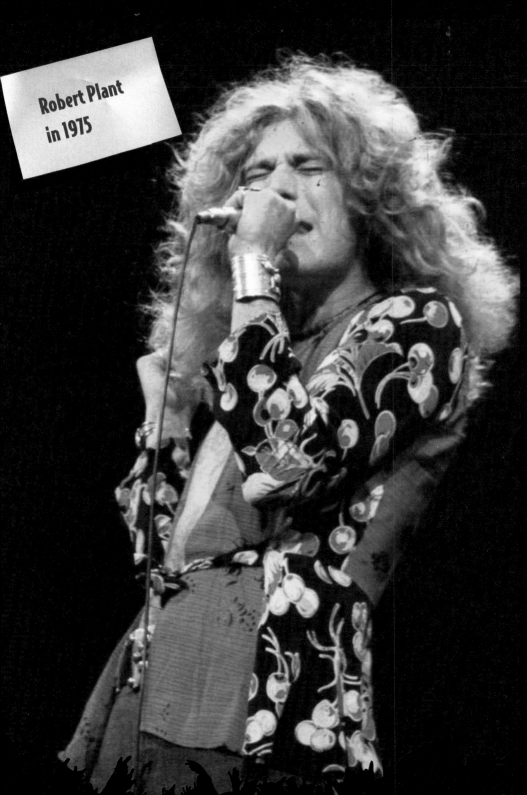

Robert Plant
in 1975

imitate Presley's best stage moves. His parents knew he loved music, so they let him test his skills. They drove him to the nearby Seven Stars Blues Club. There he would jam with a house band. While he admired Elvis, Robert best liked singing the songs of African-American blues performers such as Muddy Waters and Big Joe Williams.

However, Plant's parents insisted that he study accounting. Music was okay as a hobby, but his parents did not want him pursuing such a risky career choice. Robert dropped out of school at age sixteen and went to work for a professional accountant. If he had done what his parents wanted, Plant would have spent his life working on tax files and other financial records for businesses.

Plant could not stand accounting. After working all day with numbers, he went out nearly every night to jam with blues bands in and around Birmingham. His relationship with his parents soured.

In the mid-1960s, Plant joined several bands but stayed with each for a short time. One was called the New Memphis Bluesbreakers, even though his Birmingham home was roughly four thousand miles from Memphis, Tennessee. The band's name gave the members a link to the home of Elvis and the birthplace of rock and roll. Another band Plant sang with was called Black Snake Moan, named after a song by African-American blues performer Blind Lemon Jefferson. Yet another band Plant joined was the Crawling King Snakes, named for

a tune by another African-American blues man, John Lee Hooker.

Plant was having fun with music, but his father's words stayed with him. Robert knew it would he very hard to make a living playing music. He said, "Even the most talented singers usually don't make it. I'll give myself till the age of twenty; if I'm still struggling by then, I'll move on to something else."[7]

As he drifted from band to band, Robert became known for his unusual voice. It did not emit the deep, resonant sounds of most blues singers. His voice is high, yet it is as powerful as a runaway bus. Some have described it as a shriek, and others called it bloodcurdling. Years later Plant admitted that he was forced to shriek. He said, "The equipment was pretty inferior in those days." He added that in one concert hall "the p.a. system was miles in the air. There was no way the voice would project" without singing loudly.[8] Plant moved to the music like a wild man and that also made him hard to ignore.

In 1966, he joined a band called Listen. Listen was signed to a recording contract and released their first single. It was a cover record, or another version of a record that was already released. The song was titled "You Better Run," and it was first recorded by the American pop/blues band the Young Rascals. The Young Rascals' recording reached number 20 on the national charts in the United States.[9] However, the version by Listen sold hardly any copies.

Listen recorded two more singles. The record company tried to turn Robert into something he was not. They wanted him to sound like a pop singer to appeal to an older crowd. That was a horrible idea and both Listen records bombed. Robert joked that if his mother had not bought any records, they would not have sold any at all.

While attending a music concert by British pop band Georgie Fame and the Blue Flames, he met a young woman from a family that had immigrated to England from India. Her name was Maureen, and the two began dating regularly. Since he felt uncomfortable with his own family, Robert moved in with Maureen's.

At the same time, Plant continued drifting from one band to another. He sang lead in a group called the Band of Joy. That was a disaster from the start. It seemed he and the Band of Joy's manager were always arguing. At one point the manager told Robert he was a horrible singer and should quit the band. Robert did quit early in 1967 and the band broke up. But when he had doubts about his talents, Maureen encouraged him to keep trying.

Plant formed another group he also called Band of Joy. When that one disbanded, he formed a third group with the same name. The drummer for the third Band of Joy was a local young man named John Bonham.

To help stand out from so many other bands, Plant's group tried gimmicks. They performed with painted faces and

shot toy machine guns at each other onstage. None of the antics helped. Gigs were few and far between. Maureen helped pay the bills. Yet Robert said, "I wasn't going to give up. For a while I was living off Maureen."[10]

To help out, Robert took a job doing road construction. He got along well with the other construction workers. They referred to him as "the pop singer."

Band of Joy broke up for good and Plant and Bonham went their separate ways. Robert did not quit. He joined yet another group. It was called Hobbstweedle, inspired by the J.R.R. Tolkien trilogy *The Lord of the Rings*.

One night Hobbstweedle was playing a dance at West Midlands College of Higher Education outside Birmingham. Plant did not know it in advance but former Yardbirds Jimmy Page and Chris Dreja had shown up to check out the band. Plant then recognized Page from the Yardbirds. After the show, they got together and Jimmy asked Robert to show up for an audition a week later.

Page said, "When I auditioned him and heard him sing, I immediately thought there must be something wrong with him personality-wise, or that he had to be impossible to work with, because I just could not understand why, after he told me he had been singing for a few years already, he hadn't become a big name yet."[11]

The audition was the start of a long working relationship between Page and Plant.

John "Bonzo" Bonham

It would seem that John Bonham was born to be a drummer. He was born May 31, 1948, in Redditch, near Birmingham. His father, Jack, was a carpenter, and John grew up banging on anything around the house. He would wander into the family kitchen and bang on pots and pans. When John was about five, his father used an old coffee tin, a can of bath salts, and a loose wire to make his son his first drum set.

When he was ten, his mother bought John his first real drum. His parents saw that he took drumming very seriously. So when John was fifteen, his father bought him a complete drum set. It was a secondhand set, and parts were rusted. In spite of that, John treated it with tender loving care and played it almost every day.

Bonham quit school when he was sixteen. Bonham said, "When I left school I went into the trade with my Dad. He had a building business and I used to like it. But drumming was the only thing I was any good at, and I stuck at that for three or four years. If things got bad I could always go back to building."[12]

Bonham joined a local band called Terry Webb and the Spiders in 1964. Working for his father during the day allowed John to play at gigs at night. It was in 1964 that the Beatles rocketed to worldwide fame.

Like other British bands at the time, the Spiders copied the Beatles' style of dressing in matching outfits onstage.

John Bonham
in 1979

The Beatles wore suits that had been popular during King Edward VII's reign, from 1901 to 1910. The Spiders wore purple jackets with velvet lapels.

Like Plant, Bonham bounced from one group to another in his teens. Bonham was a powerful drummer, but Spiders' fans tended to like softer drumming. So Bonham joined another band, the Nicky James Movement. Lead singer Nicky James had an Elvis-style hip-shaking attitude. But the Nicky James Movement broke up not long afterward when they could no longer afford to pay for their instruments.

Talented as he was, Bonham had no trouble finding another band to play with. He joined one called the Senators, who released a single titled, "She's a Mod." Mods were groups of English young people who dressed in European-style clothing and liked alternative styles of art, music, and movies. The record sales were fair, but Bonham was restless. Over the next several months, he played with several other Birmingham-era bands with names such as A Way of Life, Steve Brett and the Mavericks, and Pat Wayne and the Beachcombers.

All the while, Bonham was living the life of a normal teenager. His friends gave him a nickname: Bonzo, after a British cartoon dog. John's manner reminded them of the cartoon dog's character.

One night when he was seventeen, John went to a dance where he met a girl named Pat Phillips. John and Pat dated for a while. When John was eighteen, he asked Pat to marry him. She thought twice about marrying a musician without steady work. John convinced her that he would some day hit the big time. But he added that if for some reason he did not make it, he would give up drumming. He convinced Pat to marry him and the couple moved into a fifteen-foot-long trailer.

Bonham continued playing for different bands. The Band of Joy, featuring Robert Plant, had heard all about this loud drummer nicknamed Bonzo. The Band of Joy's bass player was Paul Lockey, who later quit music and became a school-teacher. Lockey recalled, "Robert wanted Johnny Bonham so we used to end up going around at all hours to see him at gigs and say, yea, come on, join the band."[13]

After Band of Joy split up, Bonham played drums for an American singer named Tim Rose who was performing in England. A few months later, Plant tracked him down and asked him to join a new band. It featured Plant and Page and was called the New Yardbirds.

Bonham was hesitant. The Yardbirds—new or old—was a name from the past. Would people be interested in seeing a band that had seemed to have run its course? Because he had already played with Plant, Bonham decided to go for it. He joined the New Yardbirds.

John Paul Jones

Bass player John Paul Jones's real name is John Baldwin. He was born on January 3, 1946, in Sidcup, not far from London.

Unlike the other members of Led Zeppelin, John's family was a musical one. Both his parents had performed in vaudeville, which was a type of stage performance in the early 1900s that featured a series of acts which toured from town to town. From the time starting when John was just a toddler, they often took him with them when they traveled.

John's father, Joe, was a gifted piano player. In addition to touring, he played with big jazz bands and accompanied silent movies. Before movies with sound became popular in the late 1920s, movies were silent. Dialogue was presented as written words between scenes. To make the experience of watching a silent film more enjoyable, a piano player performed live in the theater. When a tragic scene was presented on the screen, the pianist performed sad-sounding music. When a chase scene was taking place, the pianist played lively music.

Joe encouraged John's interest in music. John learned piano when he was young. He also played organ at the church the Baldwin family attended. When John was about thirteen, he decided he wanted to play bass guitar. But Joe thought the bass guitar was a fad that would never last. He told John, "Don't bother with it. Take up the tenor saxophone. In two years the bass guitar will never be heard of again."[14]

However, John had his heart set on the bass. He drew bass guitars on his schoolbooks and convinced his father that bands were looking for good bass players. Once Joe found

out his son could make money playing bass guitar he gave John his blessing.

In the days before the Internet, there was only one way to pick up radio stations from across the world. That was short-wave radio. Joe had one and John loved listening to faraway radio stations. He taught himself the bass while playing along with the songs on the short-wave radio. Many musicians he admired were jazz artists who did not play electric bass guitar. Instead, they played stand-up bass, or bass violin. These included Charles Mingus, Ray Brown, and Scott LaFaro. One song John really liked was a rousing number called "You Can't Sit Down" by an American band called the Phil Upchurch Combo. Upchurch was the bass player and bandleader. John was impressed by the song's bass solo.

John went away to boarding school at about age fifteen where he formed his first band, the Deltas. By the time he was sixteen, the Deltas were playing at American military bases in England. Determined to become a professional musician, he quit school shortly afterward. Baldwin had no problem getting hired to play in several bands. And like Bonham's, Baldwin's bands wore outfits onstage that would have seemed ridiculous just a few years later. One band he played with wore purple jackets with white shoes.

Like Jimmy Page, Baldwin decided to try making a living as a session musician. And like Page, he played for a variety of headliners. From 1964 through 1968, Baldwin's bass could be

John Paul Jones in 1975

heard on songs by rockers the Rolling Stones and Jeff Beck as well as pop artists Lulu and Tom Jones.

It was also around 1964 that Baldwin took on a stage name: John Paul Jones. Different people in the music business have been given credit for convincing Baldwin to change his name. The most common story is that he simply took the name from the title of a 1959 movie about John Paul Jones, the Revolutionary War naval hero.

In 1966, Jones married a girl named Maureen, known by her friends as "Mo." Within a couple of years, they had two daughters. Jones enjoyed working in music studios since he did not have to tour and could stay home with his family. It was also in 1966 that Jones moved from session musician to music arranger. As an arranger, he planned how musicians would play on a record. Arrangers have a huge role in how a record sounds. One of the best known musical artists he arranged for was the pop band Herman's Hermits. Herman's Hermits had several hit singles from 1965 through 1968 that were popular with preteens and young teenagers.

Jones decided to release his own single in 1967. The "A" side was titled "Baja." The "B" side was "A Foggy Day in Vietnam." The record did not sell well, but bigger things were in Jones's future. He saw an advertisement in a magazine asking for a bass player for a new band. That band was the New Yardbirds.

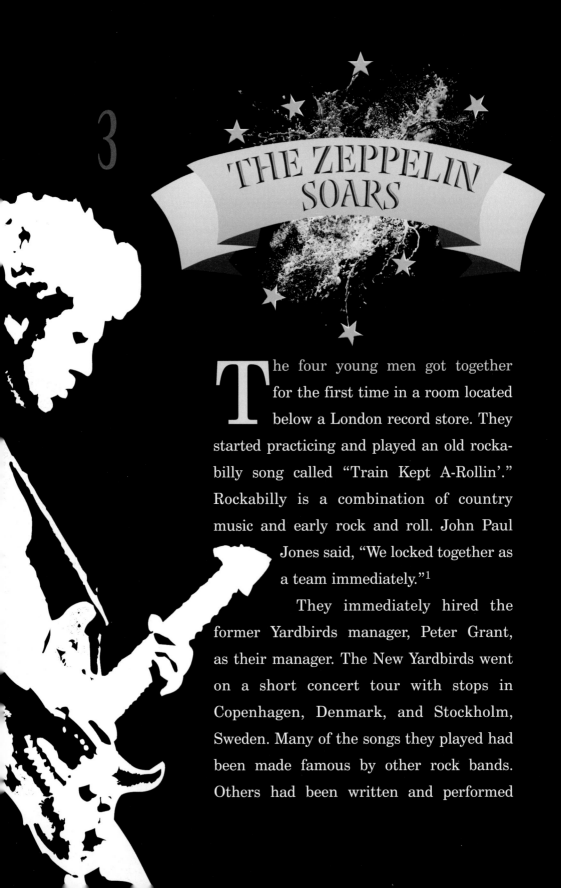

3

THE ZEPPELIN SOARS

The four young men got together for the first time in a room located below a London record store. They started practicing and played an old rockabilly song called "Train Kept A-Rollin'." Rockabilly is a combination of country music and early rock and roll. John Paul Jones said, "We locked together as a team immediately."[1]

They immediately hired the former Yardbirds manager, Peter Grant, as their manager. The New Yardbirds went on a short concert tour with stops in Copenhagen, Denmark, and Stockholm, Sweden. Many of the songs they played had been made famous by other rock bands. Others had been written and performed years earlier by blues artists. A few were products of the original Yardbirds.

However, they also experimented with original songs. One was a rocking number called "Good Times Bad Times." Another was titled "Dazed and Confused," which has a mournful, dreamlike tone. Much of the sound is a result of Page's imaginative guitar work. Like most guitarists, he usually strummed or plucked the instrument with his fingers. But on "Dazed and Confused" he played the guitar with a violin bow.

THE NEW YARDBIRDS WENT ON A SHORT CONCERT TOUR. THEY WOULD LATER CHANGE THEIR NAME TO LED ZEPPELIN.

After they returned from Scandinavia, the band decided it needed a new name. The New Yardbirds had little to do with the original Yardbirds. Only Page and Bonham had been with the original Yardbirds, and only for a short period after the group had reached its prime.

There are different versions of how the group came up with Led Zeppelin. All involve two members of the British super band, the Who.

One story says that the Who's bassist John Entwistle and drummer Keith Moon were joking around with their tour manager Richard Cole about forming a new musical group with Page. Moon supposedly said, "I've got a good name for it. Let's call it Lead Zeppelin, 'cause it'll go over like a lead balloon."[2] A zeppelin was a cigar-shaped rigid airship made in Germany. It was also known as a dirigible.

Another version says that John Entwistle said the music of the planned new group would be "so heavy it should go down like a lead zeppelin."[3]

Entwistle and Moon did not leave the Who. Whether it was meant to be taken seriously or as a joke, the name Lead Zeppelin was too good to pass up. The members of the New Yardbirds liked the sound of it. They also liked the idea of the two words together. There was something heavy (lead) mixed with something lighter than air (a zeppelin). An American heavy metal band popular at the time was called Iron Butterfly. Iron Butterfly conceived its name because of the light and heavy meaning. The guys in Led Zeppelin liked that idea.

The official band name was changed from Lead Zeppelin to Led Zeppelin for a simple reason. The band members did not want people to pronounce the first word "leed" by mistake.

Led Zeppelin first performed under their new name in England on October 15, 1968. The setting was Surrey University, near London. They played a few more gigs in England before heading to the United States. Reviews of Zeppelin's concerts by British critics were mixed. Reactions by fans were generally mixed as well.

It was also that month that they recorded their first album. Most of the songs are ones they performed on their Scandinavian tour. Page said, "I wanted Zeppelin to be a marriage of blues, hard rock, and acoustic music topped with heavy choruses—a combination that had never been done before. Lots of light and shade in the music."[4]

Amazingly, the album was recorded in only thirty hours spread out over two weeks. Most albums at the time took two hundred fifty to three hundred hours to record.[5]

While waiting for the first album to be released, Zeppelin's manager Peter Grant decided to take a chance in the United States. The band's first American concert appearance was in Denver, Colorado, on December 26, 1968. Their record label, Atlantic Records, promoted their tour heavily to radio stations and newspaper music writers.

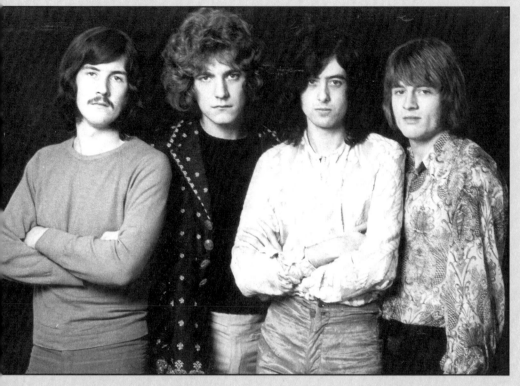

LED ZEPPELIN IN 1968, FROM LEFT TO RIGHT: JOHN
BONHAM, ROBERT PLANT, JIMMY PAGE, AND JOHN PAUL
JONES.

However, the members of Led Zeppelin were hardly stars. The headliner at the Denver concert was the hard rock American group Vanilla Fudge. Second billed was another American band, Spirit. Led Zeppelin was third billed, or the first band to play. The marquee outside the theater did not list Led Zeppelin by name. They were listed merely as "Support."[6]

A review in a Denver daily newspaper was headlined,

"Rock Concert Is Really Groovy."[7] The term "groovy" was very popular in the late 1960s and means something delightful or wonderful.

The review went on to say:

> The concert was cranked off by another heavy, Led Zeppelin, a British group making its first U.S. tour.
>
> Blues-oriented (although not a blues band) hyped-electric, the full routine in mainstream rock—done powerfully, gutstily, unifiedly, inventively and swingingly (by the end of their set).
>
> Singer Robert Plant—a cut above the average in style, but no special appeal in sound. Guitarist Jimmy Page, of Yardbirds fame—exceptionally fine. Used a violin bow on the guitar strings in a couple of tunes with resultant interesting, well integrated effects.
>
> Bassist John Paul Jones—solid, involved, contributing. John Bonham—a very, effective group drummer, but uninventive, unsubtle and unclimactic in an uneventful solo.[8]

Touring the United States was eye-opening for the British band. In England the police are not armed and people drive cars smaller than those in the United States. Plant said that in Los Angeles, it was "the first time I ever saw a cop with a gun, the first time I ever saw a 20-foot-long car."[9]

The band's long hair made them stand out. In Georgia, people went up to Page in hotel lobbies and asked him, "What kind of girl are you?" Strangers asked Plant, "Are you a boy or a girl?"[10]

The band continued touring the United States for much of that winter. It was a long, grueling tour. At times they opened for bands other than Vanilla Fudge. At one point they opened for Iron Butterfly, the American band that helped inspire their name.

On January 12, 1969, the album they had recorded in October was released. There are nine songs on it and it is titled simply *Led Zeppelin*.

The album has a very strong blues influence. That is especially true of tracks such as "How Many More Times," "You Shook Me," and "I Can't Quit You Baby." Yet what seemed to be the most played album cut on radio was "Dazed and Confused."

American audiences loved Zeppelin's concerts. That was not true of music critics. They generally blasted the group's album, even though people bought enough copies to make it a success on the national music charts. The reviewers were generally most critical of singer Robert Plant. It was hard for them to accept a blues singer with a shrill, powerful voice. The group's tour manager, Richard Cole, felt the need to protect Plant. Cole said, "I used to hide the press write-ups from him, because they were so critical. I wouldn't let him see them."[11]

The band returned to England in February. Since they had spent so much time in the United States, English audiences were not very familiar with them. So Zeppelin went on a tour of England before flying to Los Angeles on April 20.

There they began a new month-long tour of the United States. It was highly successful but near the end, Page was tired and came down with a bad case of the flu. Still, he insisted that the show went on and he played guitar as usual. He knew the band's audiences were expecting to see and hear him perform. Page told a journalist, "That's how you know you're a pro."[12]

Zeppelin spent the rest of the year playing live shows in both the United States and Europe. They spent their free time working on a second album in studios in both England and the United States. The album, titled simply *Led Zeppelin II*, was released on October 22, 1969.

Like the first album, *Led Zeppelin II* also has a heavy blues influence. Critics said that much of the music was similar to that of an African-American blues artist named Willie Dixon. One track on *Led Zeppelin II*, "Bring It on Home," was strongly compared to a Dixon song called "Bring It on Back."

The strangest track, "Whole Lotta Love," is also influenced by the music of Dixon. It starts with a guitar riff, before Plant begins wailing with his signature voice. What makes "Whole Lotta Love" most unusual is a free-form bridge lasting several minutes in the song's middle. It is a medley of odd noises, with John Bonham playing the drums and a cymbal called a high hat to keep a continuous pulsing beat. One can also hear Jimmy Page playing a guitar with a violin bow as well as soloing on a rarely heard electronic musical instrument called a theremin. All the while, Plant moans and makes other odd noises.

"Whole Lotta Love" was widely played on radio stations, but many felt the bridge did not go over well on the radio. Several stations cut the bridge when they played "Whole Lotta Love," turning a song of five and a half minutes into one just over three minutes long. Zeppelin's label, Atlantic Records, then decided to released an edited version of "Whole Lotta Love" as a single. It was released in the fall of 1969 and reached as high as number four on the national record sales chart.[13] That was unusual, however. Unlike the Beatles and the Rolling Stones, Led Zeppelin released very few singles.

Led Zeppelin was by now established as a successful and powerful band consisting of hardworking musicians. Yet they had gotten a reputation as wild partiers. That was especially true in cities where they traveled to perform live.

All the band members but Page were married. And Page had a steady girlfriend, a model named Charlotte Martin. Charlotte and Jimmy soon had a daughter they named Scarlet. Regardless, some band members saw other women when they were on the road. Some, especially John Bonham, were seriously abusing alcohol. They destroyed hotel rooms they stayed in. That included breaking lamps, television sets, and furniture. The group never made excuses for their behavior, but explained that they were blowing off steam after the intensity of their concerts. Once word got out, many people

This is Led Zeppelin in the recording studio in 1969. They were
working on what would become *Led Zeppelin II*.

felt the band members were total jerks. Of course, many hotel managers would not let the band stay in their hotels.

In addition, Page became fascinated by a British writer and philosopher named Aleister Crowley who had died in 1947. Crowley was a believer in the occult, supernatural ideas not explained by science or traditional religion. They can range from astrology to Satan worship. Page went so far as to purchase and move into the house where Crowley once lived, on the shore of Loch Ness in Scotland. When the media discussed Page's interest in Crowley, some people accused Page of engaging in Satan worship. That fueled the group's bad reputation. Page constantly denied any interest in Satan worship.

The band's appearance only added to their image. They wore their hair long and wild. To many of their fans' parents, the band looked like street thugs.

The quartet did live concerts throughout England and North America through much of 1970. By now, John Paul Jones played organ as well as bass in live shows. Zeppelin's performances consisted mostly of songs from their first two albums. However, they loved American rock and roll and often included their own arrangements of classic early American rock and roll in their shows.

So after Zeppelin played "Good Times Bad Times" and "Whole Lotta Love," they often broke into songs by Elvis Presley, Fats Domino, Little Richard, and Buddy Holly. Some of those tunes had been hits fifteen years earlier. The people

who grew up listening to Presley and Little Richard were now in their late twenties and early thirties. But most of them shunned Zeppelin's music. To them, Zeppelin was noisy and garbled. Zeppelin's fan base was college and high school students.

Tired of traveling, the band wanted a place to relax in private. They moved with their families to a rustic cottage in southern Wales called Bron-Y-Aur. The name means "golden hill" in Welsh. Bron-Y-Aur had no plumbing or electricity. The band members and their families spent cozy evenings drinking cider around the fireplace. They did not plan to turn their time at Bron-Y-Aur into a working trip. However, they did have their guitars with them and before long they were lazing around the cottage working on new songs.

Page admitted, "It was the first time I really came to know Robert. Living together at Bron-Y-Aur, as opposed to occupying nearby hotel rooms. The songs took us into areas that changed the band, and it established a standard of traveling for inspiration . . . which is the best thing a musician can do."[14]

Several songs the band composed at Bron-Y-Aur ended up on their third album, *Led Zeppelin III*. It came out on October 5, 1970. As with their first two albums, most music critics gave it a thumbs-down.

Led Zeppelin III was a departure from the first two albums. There is a greater emphasis on folk music. There is more acoustic, or nonelectric, music. One song, "Bron-Y-Aur

LED ZEPPELIN AND THEIR FAMILIES TRAVELED TO A COTTAGE
CALLED BRON-Y-AUR IN WALES TO RELAX. THE BAND SOON
STARTED WORKING ON NEW SONGS.

Stomp," has a bouncy, country feel. It is an ode by Robert
Plant to his dog, Strider. John Paul Jones plays acoustic bass,
Jimmy Page plays acoustic guitar, and drummer John Bonham
plays spoons and castanets.

Another track, "Gallows Pole," is Zeppelin's arrangement
of a centuries-old folk song; Page switched from guitar to
banjo on that number. The track "Immigrant Song" is about
the invasion of the present-day British Isles by the Vikings
over one thousand years ago. Plant wrote it because he is

fascinated by British history and legends. However, there are some basic rock songs on *Led Zeppelin III* such as "Out on the Tiles" and "Celebration Day." There is also a bluesy number, "Since I've Been Loving You."

When reviewing the album, the critics again bashed Zeppelin for being unoriginal. They said "Since I've Been Loving You" was a weak rehash of genuine American blues. Yet they also said that the acoustic and folksy tracks were poor imitations of the music of a then-popular American–British quartet, Crosby, Stills, Nash, and Young. The four Zeppelin members were so bothered by the bad reviews that they refused to talk to the music press for a year.[15] Fans bought the album, but in not as high numbers as *Led Zeppelin II*.

Yet the fans came in droves to see them play. In 1971, Zeppelin went on their first concert tour of Asia. They gave performances in Japan and Thailand. From Thailand, they flew to Bombay, India (now called Mumbai, India). Page had always been interested in Indian music and culture. While there, they visited music clubs in Bombay and jammed with local musicians. Yet one thing that stood out the most was the incredible poverty. They made friends with a man named Razark who lived in a dilapidated two-room shanty with his wife, mother, and four children.

The band left India with mixed feelings. Tour manager Richard Cole said, "It had been a hard dose of reality to see the conditions in which Razark, this thoroughly decent man, and his family lived. We certainly didn't feel guilty about our own extravagant life-style; after all, the band had worked hard for their riches. But caught up in our own way of living, it was easy to overlook the distress in the world. In Bombay, we got a tough lesson about how most of the world lives. At least for those few days in India, all of us felt their pain."[16]

They spent the rest of 1971 doing concerts, relaxing at Bron-Y-Aur, and working on their fourth album. It was released in November 1971. Surprisingly, it was not titled *Led Zeppelin IV*. In fact, it was not given any title.

On the cover is an illustration of an old man hunched over and carrying a bundle of sticks on his back. Also on the cover are four symbols. Each was designed personally by a band member. Page's comes first and seems to read "Zoso" in fancy letters. Jones's is second and looks like three connected crude fish shapes with a circle placed over them. Next comes Bonham's symbol, which is three interconnected circles. Finally, there is Plant's symbol: a circle with a feather inside it. The band members have never given clear answers to the album cover's meaning. Fans have had fun hazarding their own guesses.

Since the album has no title, people had to come up with a way to refer to it. Most call it *Led Zeppelin IV*. Others call it *Four Symbols*, *Zoso* (after the first of the four symbols), *Man With Sticks*, *Untitled*, or *Runes*. (Runes are language characters used in medieval Scandinavia.)

Reviews of the fourth album were generally better than those of Zeppelin's earlier ones, but still were mixed. But regardless of what the music critics said, the band's fans loved them. *Rolling Stone* magazine assistant editor Andy Greene said plainly, "Zeppelin was more the people's band than a critic's band."[17]

One track on the fourth album, "The Battle of Evermore," is a folksy number with acoustic guitar and mandolin. It is one of several Zeppelin songs inspired by the *Lord of the Rings* series. It is unusual in that Robert Plant shares lead vocals with a British female folk singer named Sandy Denny. Another folk-inspired number is titled "Going to California."

The fourth album also has its share of hard rock tracks. Three that received a lot of radio airplay are "Black Dog," "Misty Mountain Hop," and the appropriately named "Rock and Roll." But one song from the fourth album stands out from the others: "Stairway to Heaven." It is to this day the most requested song on FM radio stations in the United States even though it was never released as a single.[18]

Based on its first performance, one would never know it would become such a huge hit. The band introduced audiences to the song before the fourth album was released. Bassist John Paul Jones said of one audience who heard it live, "They were all bored to tears waiting to hear something they knew."[19]

While some tracks on the fourth album are folk and others are rock, "Stairway to Heaven" blends the two genres.

Page plays a double-necked guitar, showing off his versatility. The eight-minute-long song starts off slowly as an acoustic folk number. The instrumental opening has a medieval feel. About three quarters of the way through, it becomes electrified. It ends in classic heavy metal style, full of electric guitar licks.

The lyrics are mystical and people have found different meanings in them. Perhaps the most accepted interpretation is that the song is about a woman who thinks acquiring material possessions is important. Then she learns that all the material goods in the world won't get her into Heaven. Spirituality is more important than materialism. Plant later explained that when he wrote "Stairway to Heaven" he was thinking about "returning to nature, to be aware of our environment as people of long ago did."[20]

Rumors spread that playing the song backward reveals a Satanic message. Plant scoffed at the notion. He said, "I mean, who on earth would have ever thought of doing that in the first place? You've got to have a lot of time on your hands to even consider that people would do that. Especially with 'Stairway.' I mean, we were so proud of that thing, and its intentions are so positive, that the last thing one would do would be . . . I found it foul, the whole idea, you know?"[21]

The peak years of Led Zeppelin were between 1972 and 1975. In the fall of 1972 they toured the world again. After concerts in Bangkok, Thailand, they flew to Bombay, India.

Page and Plant fulfilled a dream by doing some experimental recordings with some of India's top musicians. That included members of the Bombay Symphony Orchestra. The final recordings did not live up to Zeppelin's standards, though, and were not released to the public.

In March 1973, Led Zeppelin released its fifth album. It was their first album to have a creative title: *Houses of the Holy*. The title is not about churches, synagogues, mosques, or temples. "Houses of the holy" was the band's term for the massive stadiums and arenas where they played. The album title is interpreted as a thank you to their fans who pay their hard-earned money to see them perform.

As before, Zeppelin's new album was a hit with the fans but not critics—even though it features even fewer blues touches than their earlier albums. The tracks share a variety of influences. "The Crunge" is based in African-American rhythm and blues and soul music. "D'yer Mak'er" can be described as 1950s rock and roll meets West Indian reggae. "The Rain Song" is a lengthy hard rock love ballad featuring an electronic keyboard called a mellotron played by Jones. "The Song Remains the Same" features Page's intricate guitar work.

About this time the band tried to broaden its appeal. They wanted to shed their reputation as a bunch of hotel-wrecking partiers. So manager Peter Grant hired an American public relations consultant to help change their image. The job of those who work in public relations is to help businesses or individuals become better known or develop new images. The person Grant hired was a twenty-three-year-old man with longer hair than any of the band members. His name was Danny Goldberg.

Goldberg suggested that the band ignore their bad reviews and start doing interviews with the music press. That way they could make their side known. They could stress in these interviews that they are serious musicians. Part of Goldberg's job was to send articles to newspapers, magazines, and radio and television stations. Goldberg did so with enthusiasm, even though he may have exaggerated a bit now and then. His articles gave Zeppelin ample publicity about their 1973 tour of the United States.

Zeppelin's concerts were no longer simple performances. Zeppelin was one of the earliest bands to use special effects such as lasers, reflectors, artificial smoke, and cannons in their shows. The 1973 tour began in Atlanta where forty-nine thousand fans filled Atlanta-Fulton County Stadium.[22] The next night they played before a crowd of fifty-six thousand in Tampa, Florida. That set an attendance record for the biggest single concert audience in the United States up until that time.[23]

The band played thirty-six dates that summer, and some Zeppelin concerts sold out in just four hours. This was years before the Internet was available in people's homes. Buying

tickets meant going to a stadium or arena and waiting for hours with thousands of others for the box office to open.

Yet the band was not past its partying stage. They had a wild party for John Bonham's twenty-fifth birthday in Los Angeles. George Harrison of the Beatles was a guest, and he and Bonham took part in a birthday cake fight. Several guests ended up in the hotel swimming pool. However, thanks to Goldberg, people now knew the guys in Zeppelin may have wild sides but they were superb musicians.

After a concert that summer in New York City's Madison Square Garden, more than two hundred thousand dollars of the band's money was stolen from the hotel where they were staying.[24] Goldberg's comment to reporters afterward was, "I was very pleased that it said Led Zep robbed on the front page of the *Daily News* rather than just rock band robbed. Now everyone knew they were the biggest rock band in the world."[25]

Led Zeppelin did not tour in 1974. They put their efforts into making their sixth album, which would be a double album, or two records in the same package. Because their contract with Atlantic Records had expired, the band started their own label. They called it Swan Song Records.

While in Los Angeles promoting their new label, the group took advantage of a special opportunity. Their hero, Elvis Presley, was doing a concert in town. A business associate who had worked with both Elvis and Zeppelin got the band tickets to see his show. Early in his concert, Presley announced that Led Zeppelin was in the audience. He then asked that a spotlight be shone on them. Afterward he asked to meet the group.

They met at the hotel where Presley was staying, and chatted for a while. Plant and Presley together sang an impromptu version of one of Elvis's songs, "Treat Me Like a Fool." Presley then signed autographs for the band. Then he stunned the British quartet by asking for their autographs.

Bonham was shocked and whispered to tour manager Richard Cole, "Can you believe it. Elvis wants *my* autograph."[26]

The band had even more surprising fans. The children of President Gerald Ford announced on a national television program that Led Zeppelin was their favorite musical group. Plant joked in response, "I was pleased to hear that they like our music around the White House. It's good to know they've got taste."[27]

Zeppelin's double album, *Physical Graffiti*, was released in February 1975. It includes another wide mix of musical styles. They went back to their blues roots with the longest number, "In My Time of Dying." It is based on a song by African-American blues musician Blind Willie Johnson. The keyboard-driven, hard rock track "Trampled Under Foot" was popular on FM stations. But the album became best known for "Kashmir," a haunting tune with musical influences from the Middle East and India. Zeppelin hired outside musicians to

THE BAND TOURED IN 1975 TO PROMOTE THEIR NEW ALBUM *PHYSICAL GRAFFITI*.

play brass and strings. Unlike their previous five albums, *Physical Graffiti* was praised by critics. It was also a big success commercially.

The band went on a punishing American concert tour to promote *Physical Graffiti*. Their schedule called for forty shows in twenty-six cities. It turned out to be a troubled tour. While getting out of a train, Page injured a finger on his left hand. He had to adapt his playing style, but was unable to play "Dazed and Confused." It was dropped from their repertoire. Plant picked up a severe cold that turned into the flu. The band was now heavily into illegal drug and alcohol use.

This seemed to signal the end of the band's peak popularity. Things were never going to be the same for Led Zeppelin.

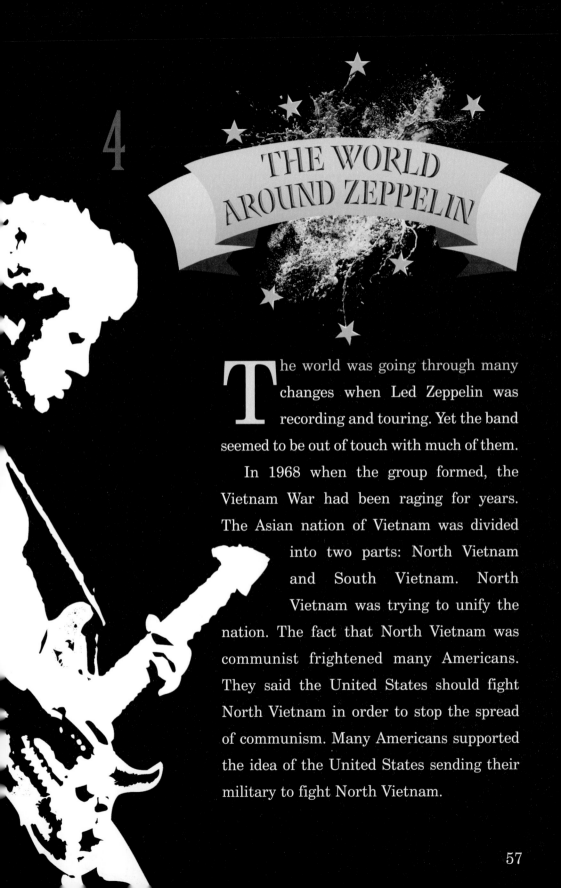

THE WORLD AROUND ZEPPELIN

4

The world was going through many changes when Led Zeppelin was recording and touring. Yet the band seemed to be out of touch with much of them.

In 1968 when the group formed, the Vietnam War had been raging for years. The Asian nation of Vietnam was divided into two parts: North Vietnam and South Vietnam. North Vietnam was trying to unify the nation. The fact that North Vietnam was communist frightened many Americans. They said the United States should fight North Vietnam in order to stop the spread of communism. Many Americans supported the idea of the United States sending their military to fight North Vietnam.

But others saw the fighting as nothing more than a civil war in another part of the world. To them the United States had no business being there. In addition, the vast majority of American soldiers were drafted into the military. That means they did not join the armed forces as volunteers. The United States government forced them to leave their jobs or schools and become soldiers.

Many Americans, especially college and high school students, protested the war. College students were especially

THE 1970s WERE TURBULENT TIMES. THERE WERE MANY PROTESTS, SUCH AS THIS ONE IN 1970, WHERE PEOPLE SPOKE OUT AGAINST THE VIETNAM WAR.

active in the protests since they were of draft age. Several made it clear that they did not disagree with all wars—just unjust ones. On the other hand, there were many against the idea of war in general.

A lot of young people in the late 1960s felt their parents' generation was at fault for the Vietnam War. They believed their parents saw war as the only answer to problems between nations. The older generation, many of whom had fought in World War II, saw Vietnam War protesters as unpatriotic. The young antiwar students rebelled by making a point to act and dress differently from their parents. They grew their hair long, and wore blue jeans rather than suits and ties. Flowers represented peace and beauty, so many wore flowers in their hair. They used illegal drugs. The most popular was marijuana.

In the world of jazz in the 1940s and 1950s, people who were cool were called "hep." By the 1960s, the word had morphed into "hip." The longhaired, antiwar generation began to refer to themselves as "hippies."

Most, but not all of the antiwar protests happened in the United States. Yet, young people in western European countries protested the same way to show sympathy for young Americans.

The soundtrack for this youth rebellion was rock music. In the early 1960s, there had been a smattering of popular protest songs by folk artists such as Bob Dylan and Joan Baez.

But most rock songs in the early 1960s were about fun topics such as young love and high school dances. When the Beatles and Rolling Stones first became popular in 1964, their songs were also about school crushes and boy-meets-girl romance.

By 1967 the Beatles began singing songs about love and peace. The love they referred to was not romance but brotherhood. Rock bands from San Francisco, the unofficial capital of the hippie movement, included the Grateful Dead and Jefferson Airplane. Many of their songs were musical protests of the Vietnam War. Other bands, such as Country Joe and the Fish; Crosby, Stills, and Nash; and the Doors followed suit. Even the light pop group, the Monkees, got into the act. They satirized their parents' generation in a 1967 song titled "Pleasant Valley Sunday."

In August 1969, a three-day concert featuring the nation's biggest artists in rock music was scheduled to take place in Bethel, New York. An audience of perhaps fifty to one hundred thousand people was expected. However, roughly a half million showed up. The audience members had a lot in common. Most had long hair. Most smoked marijuana and used harder drugs in the open. Almost all strongly opposed the Vietnam War.

The concert was officially called the Woodstock Music and Art Fair, named for a nearby town. It has since become known simply as Woodstock. It is today viewed as a landmark event of the hippie movement.

By 1970 and 1971, it seemed that every artist that received radio airplay was doing a Vietnam War protest song. Some tackled other social issues, too. Elvis Presley, who had never before put political messages in his music, was singing about the dream of world peace and the hardships of inner-city life.

The mostly African-American Motown label produced dozens of hit songs throughout the 1960s. These were catchy melodies with a rhythm and blues base. Like rock musicians of the early and mid-sixties, Motown artists such as Marvin Gaye, Stevie Wonder, the Temptations, and the Supremes sang about falling in love or being in love. By the late 1960s, they too were recording songs about political subjects such as war and urban strife.

In spite of everything that was going on around them, Led Zeppelin did no message-driven songs. Their music had no political meanings. But Zeppelin's fans of the late 1960s and early 1970s did not care.

One reason for the lack of message-driven songs by Led Zeppelin was timing. Zeppelin was a new band on the scene in the summer of 1969. They had released only one album. Most of the performers at Woodstock had been around for at least two or three years and already had big followings. In 1969, Zeppelin appealed greatly to high school-age students. They were the younger brothers and sisters of those who came of

age with the Beatles, the Rolling Stones, the Jimi Hendrix
Experience, and the Grateful Dead.

Actually, Zeppelin was offered a chance to play at
Woodstock. Peter Grant turned it down. Being a new band,
Zeppelin would have been one of the minor acts on the bill.
Grant did not want his band to be just one of many opening
bands. Some music historians today believe that if they had
played Woodstock, Zeppelin would have endeared themselves
to an audience of older rock fans.

Zeppelin's high school-age fans followed the band into
their own college years in the early 1970s. While college students in the early 1970s did embrace the Beatles, Hendrix, the
Grateful Dead, and other favorite musicians of their older siblings, Zeppelin was a band they could call their own—a band
they had come of age with. By 1973 the military draft had
ended and the United States had gradually pulled its troops
out of Vietnam. Andy Greene, assistant editor of *Rolling Stone*
magazine, said, "By the time Zeppelin was at its biggest, much
of the war was over."[1] There were fewer issues to protest.

Greene also stated that being British, Zeppelin had less of
a personal stake and less firsthand interaction with the deci-
sions made by the United States government.

On the other hand, Zeppelin appealed to young fans of
American blues. British bands such as the Rolling Stones and
the Animals had been covering American blues classics since
1964. With its louder and heavier sounds, Zeppelin took their

BY THE 1970S, LED ZEPPELIN WAS FILLING A MUSIC VOID—
AND THEY DID IT THEIR OWN WAY. THEY HAD A JET WITH
THEIR NAME ON IT TO FLY THEM ALL OVER THE WORLD.

blues base to a whole new level. And they did it without inserting political messages into their songs.

Greene said, "To Zeppelin, the purpose of a rock band is simply to entertain and make good music. Some would say to Zeppelin it was partying and playing loud music."[2]

Other observers said that Zeppelin did affect society but in a more subtle way than those who sang openly about political

issues. Ralph Hulett, coauthor with Jerry Prochnicky of *Whole Lotta Led: Our Flight With Led Zeppelin*, explained, "They had already drawn youth culture like a magnet. They, especially Jimmy Page, had no need to intensify that."[3]

Hulett said that the political turmoil made the early 1970s "a desperate decade. We [young college-age people] wanted something we could relate to. Led Zeppelin was a symbol of being anti-establishment."[4]

Hulett points out that by the early 1970s the Beatles had broken up. By that time also, rock stars Jim Morrison, Jimi Hendrix, and Janis Joplin had all suffered drug-related deaths. With those idols gone, Hulett said, "Zeppelin came and filled that void. They fanned the flame of us versus them, without really wanting to do so. They created their own rules and lived by them."[5]

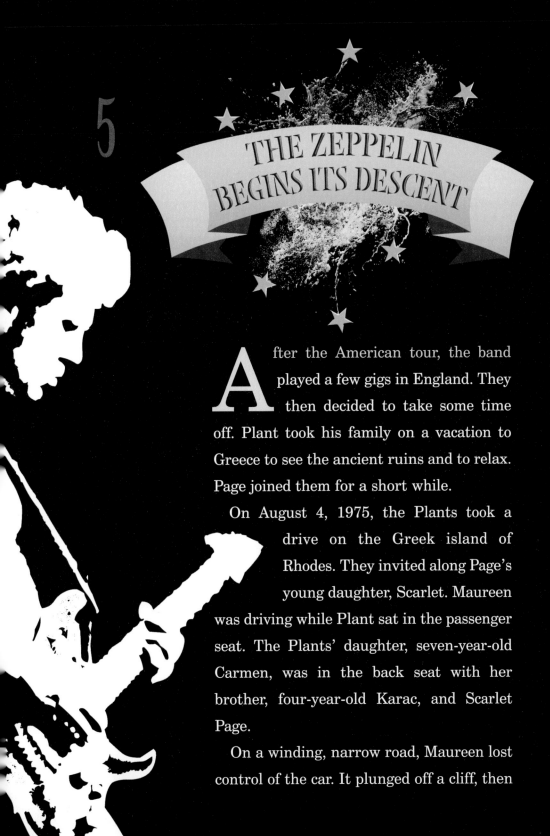

5

THE ZEPPELIN BEGINS ITS DESCENT

After the American tour, the band played a few gigs in England. They then decided to take some time off. Plant took his family on a vacation to Greece to see the ancient ruins and to relax. Page joined them for a short while.

On August 4, 1975, the Plants took a drive on the Greek island of Rhodes. They invited along Page's young daughter, Scarlet. Maureen was driving while Plant sat in the passenger seat. The Plants' daughter, seven-year-old Carmen, was in the back seat with her brother, four-year-old Karac, and Scarlet Page.

On a winding, narrow road, Maureen lost control of the car. It plunged off a cliff, then smashed into a tree. The accident happened on a remote part of the island. The five of them lay there in pain for hours. A farmer in a fruit truck eventually passed by and brought them to the closest hospital.

Scarlet suffered only some bruises, but Karac had a broken leg and Carmen a broken wrist. Plant's right elbow, right ankle, and several bones in his right leg were broken. Maureen's injuries were the worst. She had a broken leg, broken pelvis, and a fractured skull.

All were airlifted to a hospital in Rome, Italy. Then they were brought home to London. They all survived the accident, but Maureen spent several weeks healing in a hospital, and Plant was unable to walk for a half a year.

Obviously, touring was out of the question. Plant and Page flew out to Los Angeles and rented beach houses on the Pacific Ocean for further rest. The peaceful atmosphere inspired them, and it was not long before they started writing songs and practicing. Jones and Bonham joined them in Los Angeles. It was a strange scene—the band rehearsing with Plant singing from a wheelchair.

Though Plant was severely injured, in time he became more mobile. The quartet flew to Munich, West Germany, to record a new album in a place called Musicland Studios. Musicland was regarded as one of the best recording studios in Europe. Plant sang while sitting on a stool.

The band banged out the album, their seventh, in just

eighteen days.[1] Plant explained that the accident was the main reason for the rush. "It was really like a cry of survival. I didn't know whether I was going to be able to work with the band again; I didn't know if my leg would heal. We had planned to do a world tour, but obviously that was nipped in the ankle, so to speak."[2]

The new album, *Presence*, was released March 31, 1976. The cover is as cryptic as that of the fourth album. There are no runes on this one. Instead, it features a family of four straight out of the early 1960s, sitting at a table in a marina-side restaurant. There is no food on the table. Nor is there silverware or place settings. The only thing on the tablecloth is a black monolith, or freestanding object. The band members referred to it merely as "the object."

The band gave little explanation about the cover's meaning. Plant said to a reporter, "I'm glad people are wondering what it means. The most I can say is that everybody should work it out for themselves—it's not hard to work out especially for our Kubrickian fans."[3] The term "Kubrickian" refers to movie director Stanley Kubrick, who had directed the futuristic classic *2001: A Space Odyssey* just eight years earlier. A mysterious black monolith is seen several times in the movie.

When asked directly if the monolith on the album cover was inspired by *2001: A Space Odyssey*, Plant answered, "Whatever you want to say, it says it. *The Object* can be taken in many ways." He added, "But there's not much fun in knowing everything is there?"[4]

Once again, the album received mixed reviews while selling very well. The most popular songs included "Achilles Last Stand," a hard rock number featuring manic drumming by Bonham and one of Page's best-known guitar solos, and "Nobody's Fault but Mine," heavily influenced by American blues singer Blind Willie Johnson.

Later that year, the band ventured into a new medium: film. They starred in a movie titled *The Song Remains the Same*. That was also the title of a track from the album *Houses of the Holy*. The movie was first shown in New York City on October 21, 1976.

Most of the movie consists of concert footage filmed at New York's Madison Square Garden in 1973. Also included is behind-the-scenes footage. What made *The Song Remains the Same* stand out from other concert films at the time is the inclusion of five fantasy sequences. Each stars and was written by each band members and manager Peter Grant. Grant portrays himself as a gangster from the 1930s. Some critics say it symbolizes the tough attitude he has to take as a businessman in the music industry.

Plant explores his interest in the medieval age by playing a knight in armor rescuing a damsel in distress. Page fights his way up a mountaintop in Scotland and meets a wise old man with flowing hair. Jones plays a criminal who comes

In 1976, Led Zeppelin starred in their movie *The Song Remains the Same.* It featured concert footage and short fantasy sequences written

home to a warm and happy family. Bonham plays pool, rides a motorcycle, and goes drag racing.

The band's fans ate the film up, but critics were not so kind. Many had especially hard words for the fantasy sequences. They said the fantasies made the band members look as if they were a bit too full of themselves.

Although Plant was not 100 percent recovered, the band took off on another American tour in 1977. Things did not go well. The band was still heavily into drug use, and they were not getting along with each other.[5] Bonham, Page, and tour manager Richard Cole had become addicted to cocaine and heroin.[6] Both drugs are highly addictive and can harm the human body.

Cole recalled one period when some of the members and crew were heavily into drug use. "That Christmas, I was literally out of my head from regularly snorting the stuff [heroin]. One night, I became so ill at a Christmas party at Peter's house that I spent most of the evening in the bathroom, vomiting repeatedly and praying for the night to end."[7]

Bonham and Page were also suffering from the effects of their addictions. Page was jumpy and nervous. He was having aches and pains, and he seemed to have a constantly running nose.

One time the band's crew found Bonham lying in a hotel room bed, barely moving. His only action seemed to be stuffing his mouth with candy bars. Cole reported, "Bonzo looked pale, disoriented, and almost comatose. He didn't seem to be in any mood to be harassed by me. 'I couldn't get out of bed even if I wanted to,' he said. 'All I feel like doing is eating sweets.'"[8]

Cole later looked back on their addictions. He said, "I wasn't ready to admit that I had a problem, so I figured Jimmy didn't have one, either. If we had been more honest with ourselves and faced up to our addictive behavior, we might have avoided a lot of agony down the road."[9]

The tension reached a head as the band prepared to go onstage in late July in Oakland, California. Different people have their own versions of what happened.

The incident began when Peter Grant's eleven-year-old son, Warren, wanted to take a dressing room plaque that read "Led Zeppelin" as a souvenir. Some say Warren tried taking the plaque on his own. Others say Warren politely asked a stagehand for the plaque. There are also different accounts of what happened next. One is that the stagehand kindly told Warren that the plaque was needed for a show the next day. Another is that the stagehand either slapped or pushed the boy.

The story continues that Peter Grant, John Bonham, and Led Zeppelin security guard John Bindon took the stagehand inside a closed room and beat him up. Supposedly, Richard Cole stood guard at the door to make sure no one could rescue the stagehand.

When he found out about the incident, the promoter of the Oakland concert, Bill Graham, called the police. Charges of battery, or unlawfully causing physical harm to a person, were filed against Grant, Bonham, Bindon, and Cole.

Graham said about Led Zeppelin after the fight, "I could never in good conscience book them again."[10]

To the media, the Oakland incident summed up everything bad about the band. They were portrayed by the American press as drug-fueled thugs who happened to be musicians.

Bonham, Grant, Bindon, and Cole were ultimately found guilty of the charges. They received suspended jail sentences and were put on probation.

The band had several more concerts to play in other cities. Robert Plant checked into a hotel in New Orleans, their next stop. Upon arriving, he was told his wife, Maureen, was on the phone from England with an urgent message. Their six-year-old son, Karac, was violently ill with a rare respiratory infection. Two hours later, Maureen called back with the horrible news that Karac was dead. It was that sudden.

The rest of the tour was immediately canceled. The shocked Plant flew back to England and refused to speak with reporters. But his father said, "All this success and fame, what's it all worth? It doesn't mean very much when you compare it to the love of a family. They are heartbroken. Karac was the apple of my son's eye. He was a strong child,

mischievous and bright and full of life. He had never been ill before. His death seems so unreal and unnecessary."[11]

Plant went into seclusion for the rest of 1977 and much of 1978.[12] The band did not tour in 1978, and fans wondered if they would break up. By mid-spring of 1978 though, the group started to work on new songs. The album *In Through the Out Door* was recorded in late fall in a studio in Stockholm, Sweden, that was owned by the Swedish vocal group Abba. It was released to the public in August 1979. The most-played song was a sorrowful rock ballad titled "All of My Love." It was written by Plant and Jones as a tribute to Karac.

Zeppelin's die-hard fans went out and enthusiastically bought the album. However, by 1979, a new Zeppelin album was no longer a hot news item. Many mainstream music fans who were in high school when Zeppelin's first album came out felt they had outgrown the band. In fact, many were listening and dancing to disco music.

Disco is about as opposite from Led Zeppelin as one can get. Disco had its roots in melodic Motown and rhythm and blues songs. It is rhythmic and syncopated, and seems to be made just for dancing. Disco also refers to a style. Instead of jeans and T-shirts, disco fans dressed in splashy clothes—designer clothes, if they could afford them. Disco was at its peak in the late 1970s.

On the other hand, edgier high school and college-aged people in the late 1970s saw Zeppelin as old fogies from their

The cover of a program for Led Zeppelin at the Knebworth Festival in 1979

older siblings' generations. The hot new music in England and the United States was punk and new wave. This was back to basics rock and roll. The songs were brief and tight. The messages were rebellious and angry. Topics included hopelessness about the future, and anger at the political system. Led Zeppelin's songs about love, blues, and ancient mythology seemed out of touch.

One of punk rock's best known groups was the Clash. The Clash's bass player Paul Simonon said during punk's peak, "I don't have to hear Led Zeppelin—just looking at their record covers makes me want to throw up."[13]

Regardless, Zeppelin still had its core following. In August 1979, the band got together and headlined two concerts at an event called the Knebworth Festival. It was their first live performance in the United Kingdom since 1975 and was a raging hit. Over two hundred thousand Zeppelin lovers came over two weekends.[14] Though other artists were on the bill, most came to see Zeppelin.

In the summer of 1980, they played to sellout crowds of Zeppelin fanatics in Europe. Perhaps in a nod to the hot punk movement, Zeppelin did away with the lasers and smoke machines of their mid-1970s shows. Their last concert was in Berlin, Germany, on July 7, 1980. They began to discuss a new North American tour.

Those plans were halted on September 25, 1980. John Bonham died in his sleep from the effects of alcohol abuse.

The three surviving members decided not to continue as a band without Bonham. On December 4, 1980, they released a statement to the media reading: "We wish it to be known that the loss of our dear friend and the deep respect we have for his family together with the sense of undivided harmony felt by ourselves and our manager, have led us to decide that we could not continue as we were."[15]

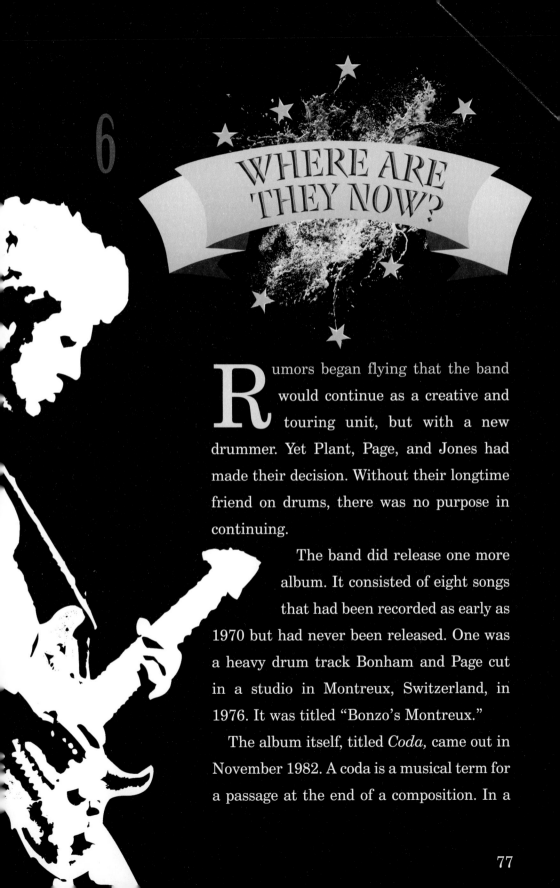

6

WHERE ARE THEY NOW?

Rumors began flying that the band would continue as a creative and touring unit, but with a new drummer. Yet Plant, Page, and Jones had made their decision. Without their longtime friend on drums, there was no purpose in continuing.

The band did release one more album. It consisted of eight songs that had been recorded as early as 1970 but had never been released. One was a heavy drum track Bonham and Page cut in a studio in Montreux, Switzerland, in 1976. It was titled "Bonzo's Montreux."

The album itself, titled *Coda,* came out in November 1982. A coda is a musical term for a passage at the end of a composition. In a way, the album was Led Zeppelin's coda capping off their career as a band. *Coda* was an appropriate finale for Zeppelin. It proved they still had loyal fans and reached number six on the top album chart.[1]

The surviving members continued their musical careers in their own ways. Plant and Page started solo careers. Plant sang in person and recorded with other backup musicians. Page got busy writing the music soundtrack for a crime movie called *Death Wish II*. In 1984, Plant and Page got together with other established musicians. One was Jeff Beck, their old guitarist friend from the 1960s. For the fun of it, they recorded a bunch of early rock and roll standards from the 1950s. They called themselves the Honeydrippers.

Two of the Honeydrippers' recordings were released on a single in 1984. One was the cover version of a rousing old rhythm and blues number called "Rockin' at Midnight." On the flip side was a dreamy ballad titled "Sea of Love." It was originally a number two hit in 1959 by rhythm and blues artist Phil Phillips and the Twilights.[2] "Rockin' at Midnight" was supposed to be the "A" side, but in the United States, radio stations played "Sea of Love" most often and turned it into a number three hit.[3]

Plant was stunned.[4] "Sea of Love" made him sound like a sentimental crooner, not a hard-rocking singer. "Rockin' at Midnight'" was later released as a single, but it did not sell as well as "Sea of Love."

Jimmy Page then became part of a band called the Firm. Lead singer Paul Rodgers had sung lead with Bad Company, a British rock band in the 1970s. Their drummer was Chris Slade, who would later play with AC/DC. The Firm released a single called "Radioactive." They toured in Europe and the United States in the mid-1980s, and recorded two albums. Neither album sold especially well, however.

John Paul Jones chose to remain behind the scenes. He opened an electronic music studio in the city of Devon, England, and taught electric composition at a British arts college. Jones put his energies into working for other artists such as R.E.M. and ex-Beatle Paul McCartney as a record producer and session musician.

In the mid-1980s, the ghost of one of Zeppelin's past successes came to haunt them. Blues veteran Willie Dixon sued the band for plagiarism. He claimed that "Whole Lotta Love" from *Led Zeppelin II* was too similar to his song "You Need Love." The case never went to trial. Dixon's and Led Zeppelin's lawyers reached a compromise decision. Dixon was paid an undisclosed amount of money for the use of his music.

Plant later said that he was not upset by the lawsuit brought by Dixon.[5] However, he explained that he was influenced by Dixon. But that fell short of stealing from him. Plant said that new music naturally evolves from music that came before it.

Plant also felt there were enough differences between

Dixon's song "You Need Love" and "Whole Lotta Love." He explained, "With the power of Jimmy Page's guitar riff and the actual 'whole lotta love' vocal line which became the chorus, and the psychedelic centerpiece . . . it was only a part of the entire effect."[6]

Plant added that a riff in Michael Jackson's hit song "Thriller" is similar to Page's riff in "Heartbreaker." But he never considered Jackson to be plagiarizing.[7]

Rolling Stone assistant editor Andy Greene said, "There was for a long time a grand tradition in music in building on what came before you."[8] However, Greene admitted that Zeppelin did borrow a lot from established blues artists in their first album.[9]

Early in 1985, Plant and Page heard about a special concert to be held July 14 that year. The event would actually be two day-long concerts—one taking place in London, the other in Philadelphia. It was part of a special charity benefit called Live Aid. Money earned from the two concerts would help fight hunger in Africa.

Page and Plant thought the time was right to play together in public again. They told Jones about their plans and he was up for it. The trio was put on the schedule as one of about twenty-five superstar acts at the Philadelphia concert.

Jones was put on keyboards, so one of Plant's current backup musicians, Paul Martinez, was hired to play bass. Tony Thompson, who had played drums in both the disco band Chic

IN 1985, LED ZEPPELIN PERFORMED AT LIVE AID IN PHILADELPHIA, PENNSYLVANIA.

and the superstar rock band Power Station, shared drumming duties with Phil Collins from British rockers Genesis. Thanks to ultrafast jet transportation, Collins pulled off an incredible feat. He played drums in the morning in London, then flew to Philadelphia where he played drums three thousand miles away on the same day.

The revitalized Led Zeppelin played three of their best-known songs: "Rock and Roll," "Whole Lotta Love," and "Stairway to Heaven." Their performance was criticized by many, including the band members themselves. Page was given an out-of-tune guitar, and Plant's voice was hoarse from performing several gigs in rapid succession before Live Aid. Collins seemed to be tired from his cross-country flight. But the crowd did not care. They were thrilled to see Led Zeppelin in concert again.

Rumors began spreading that the Zeppelin reunion would be a permanent thing. That was not to be, but the three original Zeppelin members played together again in 1988. The setting was a concert celebrating the fortieth anniversary of Atlantic Records, their original label. This time, John Bonham's son Jason played drums.

The band actually played one more time together. It was an informal session that took place at Jason Bonham's private wedding in 1990.

Jones retreated back into the recording studio while Page and Plant performed live now and then in the 1990s. Sometimes they played together at the same show; other times they played with their own backup musicians. They also released a few new albums.

In 1994, Page and Plant were given a special opportunity. While best known for loud music and spectacular concerts, this gig gave a new generation the chance to appreciate them. It also allowed their old fans to see them in a new light. They appeared on a MTV television program titled, *MTV Unplugged*. On the show, rock musicians best known for playing electrified instruments played acoustically.

Zeppelin's performances for *MTV Unplugged* had been

taped live during concerts in August 1994. The show was broadcast in October, and consisted of a dozen songs including "Battle of Evermore," "Gallows Pole," and "Kashmir." Plant and Page's renditions included accompaniment from string and other sections from the Egyptian Ensemble and the London Metropolitan Orchestra.

The next year Led Zeppelin was inducted into the Rock and Roll Hall of Fame. Then in November 1997, the first new Led Zeppelin album in fifteen years was released. It was titled *Led Zeppelin BBC Sessions* and was a two-disc set of live music the band had recorded years earlier for the British Broadcasting Company (BBC).

The music world was in for a big surprise in 1999 when John Paul Jones released his first solo album. It is called *Zooma*, and Jones plays bass, mandolin, organ, and guitar. There are no vocals; all nine songs are instrumentals.

The Led Zeppelin re-release mill continued to churn out products. A three-compact disc set titled *How the West Was Won* came out in 2003. It consists of recordings made at two June 1972 concerts in Long Beach, California. That same year, a five-hour-long, two-DVD Led Zeppelin set was released. Included was 1969 footage from a Danish TV appearance and 1979 film from their famous Knebworth Concert.

By the early 2000s, Led Zeppelin's surviving members were regarded as elder statesmen of rock. Their rousing song "Rock and Roll" was in a television advertisement for Cadillac automobiles. What made that ad especially noteworthy is that Cadillacs had always been identified with rich, stodgy, old drivers. In 1996, the average age for the owner of a Cadillac Fleetwood was sixty-seven.[10] Now Cadillac had streamlined their car designs to appeal to buyers in their fifties.

The surviving Zeppelin members were themselves middle-aged. Their core fans were as old or older. Robert Lutz, an executive of General Motors, the makers of Cadillac, said that Cadillac should be advertised only with classical music. Three other Cadillac executives convinced him otherwise. An automotive writer named Jamie LaReau answered that to middle-aged people, "Led Zeppelin is classical music."[11]

Once known for being spoiled partiers, the former band members perform today for charities. In October 2005, Plant sang with other artists in a benefit concert for victims of Hurricane Katrina. The monstrous hurricane had killed thousands and caused millions of dollars of destruction a month earlier in New Orleans and through much of the rest of mid-South. The concert raised over one million dollars.[12]

Just two months later, Jimmy Page was honored by Queen Elizabeth II for his work with poor children in Brazil. Page had noticed the poverty among street kids in Rio several years earlier when promoting an album there. He said, "I think when you're faced with a plight that's inescapable, and there's something you can do about it, you hope you can make a difference."[13]

Page worked with a British charity called Task Brazil to set up a safe house, or refuge for Brazilian kids in trouble. It has since supported over three hundred children.[14] For his efforts, the queen named Page an Officer of the Order of the British Empire.

That same year, the band received a Grammy Lifetime Achievement Award, and with it, respect from the music industry. That is amazing considering that they were snubbed by critics in their prime. Such awards are given very selectively. Having a bunch of hit records does not simply qualify an artist for this honor. National Academy of Recording Arts and Sciences (NARAS) President Neil Portnow said that Lifetime Achievement Grammys "recognize music people who have made a lasting contribution to culture around the world."[15]

Winners of Grammy Lifetime Achievement Awards include classical musicians Andres Segovia and Pablo Casals, opera singers Marian Anderson and Leontyne Price, jazz legends Louis Armstrong and Dizzy Gillespie, rock and roll pioneers Elvis Presley and Chuck Berry, country music pioneers Patsy Cline and Hank Williams, Sr., and respected pop singers Frank Sinatra and Barbara Streisand.

Led Zeppelin, the musical band that critics loved to hate, was now in very special company.

And while shunned by punk and new wave rockers decades earlier, the band has now received respect from an unusual source: hip-hop artists. Zeppelin's old songs have been sampled by the likes of the Beastie Boys and Sean Combs (P. Diddy). Page has also played live with P. Diddy.

It was on December 10, 2007, that Led Zeppelin gave their much praised charity concert for the Ahmet Ertegun Education Fund. Also in 2007, Robert Plant shocked fans by teaming up with American bluegrass/country singer and fiddle player Alison Krauss for an unusual compact disc of duets. It is titled *Raising Sand* and features remakes of country, folk, and blues classics. Plant admitted that he liked this change of pace in his musical legacy. He said, "I thought this is exactly what I want to do. I want to get away from that kind of . . . everybody's realization that I did only one thing [that] I was a one-trick pony going, 'baby, baby.' I contacted Alison and said, 'Would you like to bring your fiddle and put some life into these songs?' And we had a blast."[16]

One cut from *Raising Sand*, "Gone Gone Gone," won a Grammy Award in 2008 in the category of Best Pop Collaboration with vocals.

At the next year's awards, Plant and Krauss swept the Grammies thanks to their album, *Raising Sand*. They won five total awards. Once again Plant and Krauss won in the category of Best Pop Collaboration with Vocals. They also won in the category of Record of the Year for "Please Read the Letter," a song Plant and Page wrote together after Led Zeppelin had broken up. Finally, *Raising Sand* won the top award of the night, Album of the Year.

On December 10, 2007, Led Zeppelin hit the stage again. From left to right: John Paul Jones, Robert Plant, Jason Bonham, and Jimmy Page. Jason Bonham, son of John Bonham, played the drums.

In his acceptance speech, Plant admitted that he had changed since his first days as a rock musician. Plant said, "I'd like to say I'm bewildered. In the old days we would have called this selling out, but I think it's a good way to spend a Sunday."[17]

Although the band broke up in 1980, Led Zeppelin remains the fourth top-selling band in the United States. Only the Beatles, Elvis Presley, and Garth Brooks have sold more albums.[18]

The band's fourth album, the untitled one, is tied with Pink Floyd's *The Wall* as third best-selling album of all time. Its sales total 23 million. The album *Eagles: Their Greatest Hits, 1971–1975* is ranked first. Michael Jackson's *Thriller* is second.[19]

Andy Greene of *Rolling Stone* magazine, said, "Blues-rock isn't really in fashion today, but every kid who likes blues rock around the age of fourteen or fifteen gets into Led Zeppelin."[20] He added that Zeppelin did not linger to become a rock and roll relic. "They broke up when they were young. They are the perfect band trapped in time."[21] He added that one of Zeppelin's greatest musical legacies is that they were "one of the first bands that could really play to a huge arena, like U2 does today."[22]

Author Ralph Hulett adds that Zeppelin was the first band to have a guitar-oriented sound. He explained, "You could say the Beatles and the Rolling Stones did it, but Led

TOP: In June 2008, Alison Krauss and Robert Plant performed at a music festival in Manchester, Tennessee.

BOTTOM: In August 2008, Jimmy Page performed with British pop star Leona Lewis during the closing ceremony for the Beijing 2008 Olympics.

Zeppelin took it to a whole new level. Groups like Guns N' Roses, Lynyrd Skynyrd, and Van Halen took it forward."[23]

Hulett further credits Zeppelin for merging different types of music into their form of rock. Hulett commented, "Aside from blues, they used reggae, doo-wop, soul, and influences from the East."[24]

In their day, Zeppelin's musical genre was referred to as hard rock. That was before the term "heavy metal" was commonly used. Music historians today debate whether Zeppelin's music was indeed hard rock or an early form of heavy metal. And if it was heavy metal, did Zeppelin do it first? Or did Black Sabbath?

Rock historian Stephen Thomas Erlewine wrote plainly, "Led Zeppelin was the definitive heavy metal band."[25] He added, "More than any other band, Led Zeppelin established the concept of album-oriented rock, refusing to release popular songs from their albums as singles. In doing so, they established the dominant format for heavy metal, as well as the genre's actual sound."[26]

Dave Grohl of the bands Nirvana and Foo Fighters, wrote, "Heavy metal would not exist without Led Zeppelin, and if it did, it would (stink)."[27] Grohl also said, "They [Led Zeppelin] were never critically acclaimed in their day, because they were too experimental and too fringe."[28]

Being ahead of one's time is a statement most any artist would take as a compliment.

TIMELINE

1968—Band forms as the New Yardbirds and tours Europe; changes name to Led Zeppelin; hires Peter Grant as manager.

1968–1969—First United States tour December 1968 into February 1969.

1969—Album *Led Zeppelin* is released January 12; album *Led Zeppelin II* is released October 22.

1970—First spend time at Welsh retreat Bron-Y-Aur; album *Led Zeppelin III* is released October 5.

1971—Band makes first trip to India; album officially untitled but known as *Led Zeppelin IV* is released November 8.

1973—Album *Houses of the Holy* is released March 28; band hire Danny Goldberg as public relations consultant.

1974—Starts own record label, Swan Song Records.

1975—Double album *Physical Graffiti* is released February 24; Robert Plant, his wife, and their children are seriously injured in auto accident in Greece August 4.

1976—Album *Presence* is released March 31; movie *The Song Remains the Same* debuts in New York City on October 21; *The Song Remains the Same* soundtrack album is released October 22.

1977—John Bonham and staff members are arrested for battery in Oakland, California; Plant's son, Karac, dies.

1978—Plant begins year in seclusion; bands begins work on last album of entirely new material in mid-spring.

1979—*In Through the Out Door* is released August 15; two notable concerts at Knebworth Festival in England.

1980—John Bonham dies on September 25; band officially announces breakup on December 4.

1982—Album of previously recorded but unreleased material, *Coda*, is released November 19.

1995—Inducted into Rock and Roll Hall of Fame.

1997—Two-compact disc set *Led Zeppelin BBC Sessions* released in November.

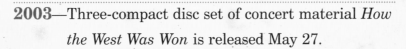

2003—Three-compact disc set of concert material *How the West Was Won* is released May 27.

2005—Receives Grammy Lifetime Achievement Award.

2007—Surviving members reunite for tribute concert to Atlantic Records founder Ahmet Ertegun on December 10.

2008—Robert Plant and Alison Krauss win Grammy award in the category of Best Pop Collaboration with Vocals; Jimmy Page performs with Leona Lewis during the closing ceremony for the Beijing 2008 Olympics.

2009—Robert Plant and Alison Krauss win five Grammy awards including Best Pop Collaboration with Vocals, Record of the Year, and Album of the Year: *Raising Sand*.

SELECTED LED ZEPPELIN DISCOGRAPHY

(Years indicate U.S. releases.)

1969 *Led Zeppelin*

Led Zeppelin II

1970 *Led Zeppelin III*

1971 fourth album, untitled

1973 *Houses of the Holy*

1975 *Physical Graffiti* (double album)

1976 *Presence*

The Song Remains the Same (soundtrack, double album)

1979 *In Through the Out Door*

1982 *Coda*

1997 *BBC Sessions* (double compact disc set)

2003 *How the West Was Won* (triple compact disc set)

CONCERT TOURS

1968 First European tour (as the New Yardbirds)

1968–1969 First American tour

1969 Second European tour

Second American tour

First United Kingdom tour

Third American tour

Fourth American tour

1970 Second United Kingdom Tour

Third European tour

Fifth American tour

Sixth American tour

1971 Third United Kingdom tour

Seventh American tour

First Japanese tour

Fourth United Kingdom tour

1972 Asian-Australia tour

Eighth American tour

Second Japanese tour

1972–1973 Fifth United Kingdom tour

1973 Fourth European tour

Ninth American tour

1975 Tenth American tour

1977 Eleventh American tour

1980 Fifth European tour

GLOSSARY

acoustic—Music played without electric amplification.

arranger—One who sets the style of a musical performance or changes an existing musical piece or song to fit a new sound or style.

blues—Music with roots in African-American culture based on a twelve-bar structure, with themes of hard times or heartbreak.

disco—Rhythmic and syncopated dance music with a strong bass line.

folk music—Traditional music emphasizing acoustic string instruments, with themes of the common working man.

"45" or single—A two-sided vinyl record with one song on each side that is played at forty-five revolutions per minute.

gig—A performing job for a musician.

hard rock—Heavily electrified rock music with strong amplification.

heavy metal—Very loud, amplified rock music, usually with loud drums and intricate guitar solos.

hippies—Young people in the late 1960s and early 1970s who were opposed to the Vietnam War and other conservative causes and who often wore long hair and embraced anti-middle-class values.

jam—To play music unrehearsed and without any preparation.

manager—One who conducts a musician's business matters.

punk rock—Basic rock music without elaborate production with themes of anger or alienation.

rockabilly—A musical form with elements of both traditional country and early rock and roll.

session musician—A musician hired to play backup for a more established musical artist.

theremin—An electronic keyboard instrument played by moving one's hands near its two antennas.

CHAPTER NOTES

Chapter 1. "The Greatest Moment of My Life"

1. Simon Cosyns, "I'm Humbled by Fans' Reaction," *The Sun*, December 7, 2007, <http://www.thesun.co.uk/sol/homepage/showbiz/sftw/article554296.ece> (December 10, 2007).

2. Peter Sorel-Cameron, "Can Led Zeppelin Still Rock?" *CNN.com/entertainment*, December 9, 2007, <http://www.cnn.com/2007/SHOWBIZ/Music/12/09/led.zep/index.html> (December 10, 2007).

3. Laura Roberts and Lucretia Munro, "Whole Lotta Herb Tea of Led Zeppelin's Stairlift to Heaven," *Daily Mail*, December 11, 2007, <http://www.dailymail.co.uk/pages/live/articles/ showbiz/showbiznews.html?in_article_id=501003&in_page_id=1773> (December 11, 2007).

4. Will Pavia, "The Hottest Ticket in Town," *The Times of London*, December 10, 2007, <http://entertainment.timesonline.co.uk/tol/arts_and_entertainment/music/article3026190.ece> (December 10, 2007).

5. Cosyns.

6. Ben Ratliff, "Led Zeppelin Finds Its Old Power," *The New York Times*, December 10, 2007,

<http://www.nytimes.com/2007/12/10/arts/music/
11zeppelin.html> (December 11, 2007).

7. Hamish MacBain, "Led Zeppelin Reunion:
The Review," *NME.COM*, December 10, 2007,
<http://www.nme.com/news/led-zeppelin/33079>
(December 11, 2007).

8. Alexis Petridis, "Led Zeppelin," *The Guardian*,
December 11, 2007, <http://www.guardian.co.uk/uk/
2007/dec/11/rock.liverockreviews> (December 11,
2007).

9. "Led Zeppelin Return to the Stage," *BBC
World*, December 11, 2007, <http://news.bbc.co.uk/2/
hi/entertainment/7135200.stm> (December 11, 2007).

10. Ibid.

Chapter 2. In the Band

1. "Interviews," Guitar Player, July 1977, <http://
www.led-zeppelin.org/reference/index.php?m=int23>
(June 11, 2007).

2. "Expelled for Elvis Haircut," newspaper clip,
displayed at Graceland, photographed August 8,
2006.

3. "Interviews," *Guitar Player*.

4. Nick Kent, "The Page Memoirs," *Achilles Last
Stand*, originally appeared in *Creem*, May 1974,
<http://www.led-zeppelin.org/reference/index.php?m
=int19> (June 11, 2007).

5. Richard Cole, *Stairway to Heaven: Led Zeppelin* (New York: HarperPaperbacks, 1992), pp. 32–36.

6. "Interview with Robert & Jimmy," *Achilles Last Stand*, January 1975, <http://www.led-zeppelin.org/reference/index.php?m=int20> (June 11, 2007).

7. Cole, p. 16.

8. Terry Gross radio interview with Robert Plant, "Fresh Air," *NPR music*, originally aired January 22, 2004, <http://www.npr.org/templates/story/story.php?storyId=1611561> (October 1, 2007).

9. Joel Whitburn, *The Billboard Book of Top 40 Hits* (New York: Billboard Books, 2004), p. 518.

10. Paul Kendall, ed. by, *Led Zeppelin: In Their Own Words* (New York: Omnibus Press, 1981), p. 14.

11. Stephen Davis, *Hammer of the Gods* (New York: William Morrow and Company, Inc., 1985), p. 60.

12. Kendall, p. 15.

13. "Band of Joy interview," *Achilles Last Stand*, 1992, <http://www.led-zeppelin.org/reference/index.php?m=int15> (June 11, 2007).

14. Davis, p. 52.

Chapter 3. The Zeppelin Soars

1. Mikal Gilmore, "The Long Shadow of Led Zeppelin," originally appeared in *Rolling Stone*, August 10, 2006, EBSCOhost, <http://web.ebscohost.com/ehost/detail?vid=9&hid= 17&sid=d532dff0-

7434-4d01-821e-d1909015403d%40sessionmgr2>
(June 12, 2007).

2. Richard Cole, *Stairway to Heaven: Led Zeppelin* (New York: HarperPaperbacks, 1992), p. 48.

3. Alan Clayson, *The Origin of the Species: Led Zeppelin: How, Why, and Where It All Began* (Surrey, England: Chrome Dreams, 2006), p. 175.

4. Ralph Hulett and Jerry Prochnicky, *Whole Lotta Led: Our Flight with Led Zeppelin* (New York: Citadel Press, 2005), p. 47.

5. Ibid., p. 46.

6. Austin Scaggs, "Q&A: Robert Plant," originally appeared in *Rolling Stone*, May 19, 2005, EBSCOhost, <http://web.ebscohost.com/ehost/detail?vid=4&hid=107&sid=3b1c880d-79d4-4726-935f-6b25a7976306%40sessionmgr104> (June 24, 2007)

7. Thomas MacCluskey, "Rock Concert Is Real Groovy," *Achilles Last Stand*, originally appeared in *Rocky Mountain News*, December 28, 1968, <http://www.led-zeppelin.org/reference/index.php?m=int1> (June 7, 2007).

8. Ibid.

9. Cameron Crowe, "Led Zeppelin," originally appeared in *Rolling Stone*, October 15, 1992, EBSCOHost, <http://web.ebscohost.com/ehost/detail?vid=9&hid=107&sid=3b1c880d-79d4-4726-935f-6b25a7976306%40sessionmgr104> (June 12, 2007)

10. "1970 North American Tour—Cops Move In," *Achilles Last Stand*, n.d., <http://www.led-zeppelin.org/reference/index.php?m=int2> (June 11, 2007).

11. Stephen Davis, *Hammer of the Gods* (New York: William Morrow and Company, Inc., 1985), p. 83.

12. Ibid., p. 100.

13. Joel Whitburn, *The Billboard Book of Top 40 Hits* (New York: Billboard Books, 2004), p. 361.

14. Ritchie Yorke, *Led Zeppelin: The Definitive Biography* (Lancaster, Pa.: Underwood-Miller, 1993), p. 110.

15. Davis, pp. 141–142.

16. Cole, p. 224.

17. Personal interview with Andy Greene, October 3, 2007.

18. "Sold on Song: Stairway to Heaven Led Zeppelin," *BBC*, <http:// www.bbc.co.uk/radio2/soldonsong/songlibrary/indepth/stairway.shtml> (September 17, 2007).

19. Ibid.

20. Terry Gross radio interview with Robert Plant, "Fresh Air," *NPR*, originally aired January 22, 2004, <http://www.npr.org/templates/story/story.php?storyId=1611561> (October 1, 2007).

21. J. D. Considine and N. Preston, "Led Zeppelin," originally appeared in *Rolling Stone*, September 20, 1990, EBSCOhost, <http://web.ebscohost.com/ehost/detail?vid=27&hid= 17&sid=d532dff0-7434-4d01-

821e-d1909015403d%40sessionmgr2> (June 12, 2007).

22. "Led Zep Rule the U.S. in 1973," *Rolling Stone*, June 24, 2004, <http://www.rollingstone.com/ artists/ledzeppelin/articles/story/6085498/led_zep_ rule_the_us_in_1973> (September 18, 2007).

23. Ibid.

24. Ibid.

25. Ibid.

26. Cole, p. 315.

27. Crowe, "The Durable Led Zeppelin."

Chapter 4. The World Around Zeppelin

1. Personal interview with Andy Greene, October 3, 2007.

2. Ibid.

3. Personal interview with Ralph Hulett, October 3, 2007.

4. Ibid.

5. Ibid.

Chapter 5. The Zeppelin Begins Its Descent

1. "Lion Among Zebras," *Achilles Last Stand*, originally appeared in *Circus* magazine, 1976, <http:// www.led-zeppelin.org/reference/index.php?m=int10> (June 11, 2007).

2. Ibid.

3. Dave Lewis, *Led Zeppelin: The 'Tight But Loose' Files* (London: Omnibus Press, 2003), p. 43.

4. Ibid.

5. Richard Cole, *Stairway to Heaven: Led Zeppelin* (New York: HarperPaperbacks, 1992), pp. 372–380.

6. Ibid., p. 365.

7. Ibid.

8. Ibid.

9. Ibid., p. 301.

10. "1977 Tour Ends in Tragedy," *Achilles Last Stand*, 1977, <http://www.led-zeppelin.org/reference/index.php? m=int11> (June 11, 2007).

11. Ralph Hulett and Jerry Prochnicky, *Whole Lotta Led: Our Flight with Led Zeppelin* (New York: Citadel Press, 2005), p. 219.

12. "Artist Biography: Led Zeppelin," *Billboard*, n.d., <http://www.billboard.com/bbcom/bio/ index.jsp?pid=5047> (June 6, 2007).

13. Brian Hiatt, "Zep Eternal: Why Is Led Zeppelin Still Popular?" *Rolling Stone*, July 28, 2006, <http://www.rollingstone.com/artists/ledzeppelin/articles/story/10962851/ zep_eternal_why_is_led_zeppelin_still_popular> (June 7, 2007).

14. "Knebworth: The Stately Home of Rock," *Knebworth House*, 2001, <http://www.knebworthhouse.com/rock/the70s.htm> (September 27, 2007).

15. Keith Shadwick, *Led Zeppelin: The Story of a Band and Their Music: 1968–1980* (San Francisco: Backbeat Books, 2005), p. 303.

Chapter 6. Where Are They Now?

1. Listings courtesy of *Billboard*, *Allmusic.com*, 2006, <http://wm04.allmusic.com/cg/ amg.dll?p= amg&searchlink=[LED|ZEPPELIN[&sql=11: wifexqe5ldde~T5> (October 2, 2007).

2. Joel Whitburn, *The Billboard Book of Top 40 Hits* (New York: Billboard Books, 2004), p. 491.

3. Ibid., p. 291.

4. Ritchie Yorke, *Led Zeppelin: The Definitive Biography* (Lancaster, Pa.: Underwood-Miller, 1993), p. 251.

5. Terry Gross radio interview with Robert Plant, "Fresh Air," *NPR music*, originally aired January 22, 2004, <http://www.npr.org/templates/ story/story.php?storyId=1611561> (October 1, 2007).

6. Ibid.

7. Ibid.

8. Personal interview with Andy Greene, October 3, 2007.

9. Ibid.

10. Jean Halliday, "Caddy Goes 'Rock and Roll,'" originally appeared in *Advertising Age*, February 4, 2002, EBSCOhost, <http://web.ebscohost.com/ehost/ detail?vid=10&hid=107&sid=3b1c880d-79d4-4726-

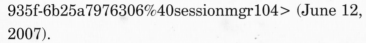

935f-6b25a7976306%40sessionmgr104> (June 12, 2007).

11. Jamie LaReau, "Who Really Picked Led Zeppelin?" originally appeared in *Automotive News*, July 11, 2005, EBSCOhost, <http://web.ebscohost. com/ehost/detail?vid=10&hid=107&sid=3b1c880d-79d4-4726-935f-6b25a7976306%40sessionmgr104> (June 12, 2007).

12. Sylvie Simmons, "This Is Very Present Tense," *The Guardian*, October 14, 2005, <http:// arts.guardian.co.uk/filmandmusic/story/0,,1591180, 00.html> (July 31, 2007).

13. Associated Press, "Queen Honors Led Zeppelin's Jimmy Page," *USA Today*, December 14, 2005, <http://www.usatoday.com/life/people/2005-12-14-queen-jimmy-page_x.htm> (July 31, 2007).

14. Ibid.

15. "Led Zep for Grammys," *UltimateGuitar.com*, February 10, 2005, <http://www.ultimate-guitar.com/ news/general_music_news/led_zep_for_grammys. html? 200502100544> (October 2, 2007).

16. Charlie Rose interview with Robert Plant, Alison Krauss, and T-Bone Walker, from PBS television show *Charlie Rose*, originally aired November 14, 2007, <http://www.charlierose.com/ guests/alison+krauss> (November 29, 2007).

17. 2009 Grammy Awards televised broadcast, John Cossette Productions, aired February 8, 2009.

18. "Top Selling Artists," *Recording Industry Association of America*, n.d., <http://www.riaa.com/goldandplatinumdata.php?table=tblTopArt> (September 30, 2007).

19. "The Recording Industry Association of America's Top Selling Albums of All Time," January 3, 2008, <http://www.infoplease.com/ipea/A0151020.html> (February 26, 2008).

20. Personal interview with Andy Greene, October 3, 2007.

21. Ibid.

22. Ibid.

23. Personal interview with Ralph Hulett, October 3, 2007.

24. Ibid.

25. Stephen Thomas Erlewine, "Led Zeppelin," *Billboard*, n.d., <http://www.billboard.com/bbcom/bio/index.jsp?pid=5047&cr=artist&> (June 7, 2007).

26. Ibid.

27. Dave Grohl, "The Immortals-The Greatest Artists of All Time: 14) Led Zeppelin" *Rolling Stone*, April 15, 2004, <http://www.rollingstone.com/news/story/5940050/14_led_zeppelin> (June 7, 2007).

28. Ibid.

FURTHER READING

Books

Crampton, Luke. *Rock and Roll: Year by Year*. New York: DK Adult, 2005.

George-Warren, Holly. *Shake, Rattle & Roll: The Founders of Rock & Roll*. Boston: Houghton-Mifflin, 2001.

George-Warren, Holly, and Patricia Romanowski, *Rolling Stone Encyclopedia of Rock & Roll*. New York: Rolling Stone Press, 2001.

Krull, Kathleen. *The Book of Rock Stars: 24 Musical Icons That Shine Through History*. New York: Hyperion Books for Children, 2003.

Schlesinger, Ethan. *Led Zeppelin*. Bromall, Penn.: Mason Crest Publishers, 2007.

Internet Addresses

Led Zeppelin Official Website
<http://www.ledzeppelin.com/>

Rock and Roll Hall of Fame and Museum
<http://www.rockhall.com>

INDEX